6/95

YOU
ARE THE
SUPREME COURT
JUSTICE

GREAT DECISIONS

YOU
ARE THE
SUPREME COURT
JUSTICE

Nathan Aaseng

The Oliver Press, Inc.
Minneapolis

The Oliver Press
Josiah King House
2709 Lyndale Avenue South
Minneapolis, MN 55408

Library of Congress Cataloging-in-Publication Data

Aaseng, Nathan.
You are the supreme court justice / Nathan Aaseng.

p. cm. — (Great decisions)
Includes bibliographical references and index.
ISBN 1-881508-14-5 : $14.95
1. United States. Supreme Court—Juvenile literature. 2. Judicial process—United States—Juvenile literature. 3. Political questions and judicial power—United States—Juvenile literature. [1. United States. Supreme Court. 2. Judicial process.] I. Title. II. Series.
KF8742.Z9A18 1994
347.73'26—dc20
[347.30735]   93-46307
                                                      CIP
                                                      AC

ISBN 1-881508-14-5
Great Decisions III
Printed in the United States of America

99 98 97 96 95 94   8 7 6 5 4 3 2 1

CONTENTS

The responsibility of interpreting the U.S. Constitution falls on the shoulders of the justices of the Supreme Court. But, as Chief Justice Charles Evans Hughes (1862-1948) pointed out, the Court can interpret the Constitution however it sees fit.

INTRODUCTION

A political storm is coming right at you. It has been building up across the nation for months, perhaps even years. One group of people demands that the laws reflect its views. Another group demands that the opposite views prevail. Fueled by passion and conviction, these two sides engage each other in furious debate. Only one institution can settle the legal squall before it spins out of control: the United States Supreme Court. You are a justice sitting on that Court.

The legal issues that come before the Supreme Court can be some of the most difficult, emotional, and explosive in the land. Some of these issues pit an individual's rights against the government's rights or the rights of states against the rights of the federal government. These issues cannot be settled to everyone's satisfaction, but *someone* has to have the final say concerning the laws in this country. You, along with eight other justices, are that someone.

The United States Supreme Court listens to appeals from those who have lost their cases in state courts (which deal with state laws) or federal courts (which deal with federal laws). Each Supreme Court justice reaches a decision in the case, and whatever the majority agrees on becomes the final say regarding the law in this country. Both the majority and the minority may explain the reasoning behind their decisions in a written opinion.

You are one of the nine Supreme Court justices. You will listen to arguments on some very difficult issues and then make a decision. Once you have reached a decision, you will learn what the real Supreme Court decided, why it reached that decision, and what impact that decision had on society. You have only three guidelines to help you solve these knotty problems: the U.S. Constitution, legal precedents, and your own principles of justice. The founders of the United States wrote the Constitution to spell out the basic laws of the nation. Unfortunately, the Constitution is not a solution to all your problems. As Chief Justice Charles Evans Hughes once said, "The Constitution is what the judges say it is."

First, there are three basic ways to interpret the U.S. Constitution. Some justices use nothing but the *exact words* that are written in the Constitution to help them decide questions of law. Others try to determine the *intent* of the writers of the Constitution. Still others believe that the Constitution is a *living document.* They insist that the framers of the Constitution could not have anticipated changes in society and that the document must be continually adapted to meet modern needs. As a

Supreme Court justice, you must decide which of those three methods you will use.

Second, you will consider legal precedents, previous decisions that courts have rendered. The legal system depends on judges abiding by precedents. If judges do not, an act that is legal today may become illegal next year. Then, no one could be certain what is truly legal; chaos and uncertainty would reign. On the other hand, judges have been known to make errors. You will have to walk the fine line between upholding precedents and correcting mistaken judgments of the past.

Third, you will rely on your own principles of justice. Sometimes neither the Constitution nor legal precedent offers any clear guidelines that will help you judge a particular case. This will force you to rely on your own sense of fairness.

Remember, your job is not to *make* laws or decide if laws are wise. Instead your job is to decide whether existing laws are legal under the Constitution. You decide cases according to the law, even if your decision is not popular with the country. Consider the arguments carefully! The decisions you make as a Supreme Court justice not only affect the individuals in each case, but also direct the course of the United States.

From within the walls of the U.S. Supreme Court building, nine justices decide whether lower-court rulings are constitutional and, in doing so, set the legal parameters for the United States government.

1

FREEDOM OF SPEECH
SCHENCK V. UNITED STATES
1919

In 1917, the United States took the grave step of entering World War I, a major conflict that pitted the country against European military powers such as Germany. Because of the risks involved in the war, American leaders took extraordinary measures to protect the country from possible harm. One of these measures required that all eligible young men be subject to conscription, commonly known as the draft. Anyone selected to serve in the nation's military forces had to answer the call or risk imprisonment.

Also in 1917, the U.S. Congress enacted the Espionage Act, which made it illegal to try to persuade people to resist joining the armed services.

The Socialist party in the United States opposed American involvement in the war. Its members believed that the draft was unconstitutional. One of the Socialist party headquarters had 15,000 leaflets printed and distributed them to men who were waiting to be sworn into the armed forces.

With impassioned language, these leaflets urged the recruits to resist the draft by any lawful means. The leaflet text compared the draft to slavery and claimed that the Thirteenth Amendment outlawing "involuntary servitude" made the draft unconstitutional. "Will you let cunning politicians and a mercenary capitalistic press wrongly and untruthfully mold your thoughts?" asked the leaflets. They urged readers to work to get the draft laws repealed through legal means.

Charles Schenck was a Socialist party official in the office that distributed the leaflets. He was prosecuted in federal court under the Espionage Act for conspiracy to cause insubordination in the armed forces and for obstructing the recruitment and enlistment of soldiers. The court convicted him and sentenced him to six months in jail. Schenck has appealed the ruling on the grounds that it violates his guaranteed right of free speech.

LEGAL HISTORY

The founders of the United States government believed strongly that people did not exist to serve government officials, but rather that the government existed to serve the people. Following the American Revolution, political leaders of several states were so concerned with protecting individual freedoms from the power of government that they refused to adopt the Constitution unless it included a Bill of Rights. This document would spell out the rights that the federal government would guarantee to the citizens of this new country.

The American people ratified the Bill of Rights as the first ten amendments to the Constitution. The *Schenck* case concerns the portion of the First Amendment that says, "Congress shall make no law . . . abridging the freedom of speech." Prior to Schenck's appeal, the Supreme Court had not clarified the meaning of this clause simply because the Court has not had the opportunity to consider a case directly concerned with freedom of speech.

YOU ARE A JUSTICE ON THE U.S. SUPREME COURT.

You must consider the arguments and decide among the options set before you.

Option 1 Declare the Espionage Act unconstitutional and free Schenck.

The Espionage Act, under which the federal court convicted Schenck, is clearly a violation of the First Amendment. James Madison, the author of that amendment, made his intentions clear. His goal was to prevent "the ambitious hope of making laws for the human mind." He believed that all people had a right to hold and express their own beliefs without the threat of government interference.

James Madison (1751-1836), the fourth president of the United States and one of the drafters of the U.S. Constitution, believed that liberty cannot exist unless people are free to disagree.

To that end, the language of the amendment is straightforward and uncomplicated. It says that Congress shall make *no law* abridging the freedom of speech. This does not merely protect popular opinions. It protects *all* kinds of speech.

Yet Congress has passed this Espionage Act with the specific intention of abridging freedom of speech. This law declares that certain types of speech—namely speech that opposes the government's action in declaring war or that supports overturning the draft—are illegal.

The role of the judiciary in the American system is to protect the rights of citizens from governmental abuse. Schenck was clearly a victim of an unconstitutional law. You should declare the Espionage Act illegal and set Schenck free.

Option 2 **Uphold Schenck's conviction.**

The *Schenck* case is an issue of conflicting rights, since there is more at stake here than simply the right of individual expression. Madison's ideal of free speech may be a proper standard during ordinary times, but these are not ordinary times. The United States is engaged in a war, and warfare presents unique dangers. All citizens of the republic have a personal stake in the outcome of the fighting. Loss of a war can pose enormous burdens on a nation. It can even destroy a nation and the lives of its citizens.

Those who hamper the war effort are aiding the enemy. They pose a threat to the "life, liberty, and pursuit of happiness" promised to all U.S. citizens. When the interests of all the people come in conflict with the interests of an individual, the government has a duty to protect the greater interest. A person's right to free speech ends when that speech becomes a danger to other citizens. Thus, the government has every right to protect its citizens by curtailing speeches and activities that might contribute to the nation's defeat. For this reason, the Espionage Act is lawful according to the Constitution and must be allowed to stand.

As the senior party member involved in the printing and distribution of the leaflets to draft inductees, Charles Schenck bore responsibility for these leaflets. His purpose in passing out this material was twofold: 1) to promote insubordination in those who were being inducted into the United States armed forces, and 2) to disrupt the American war effort by cutting off the United States' supply of soldiers. Both purposes pose a real danger to

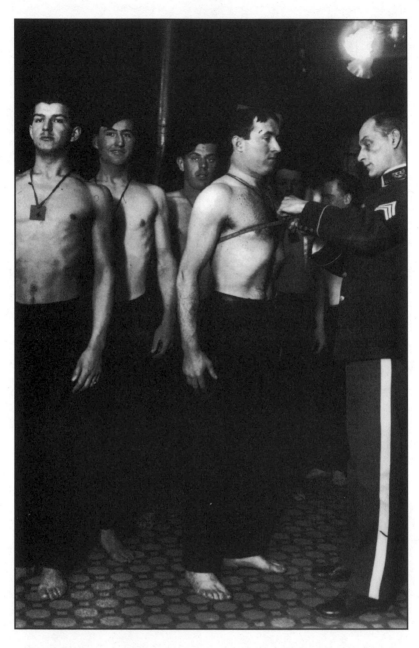

Enlisted men are examined at a New York recruiting office during World War I.

the country. If Schenck succeeded in achieving his aims, the United States would be militarily crippled and unable to defend its interests.

In this case, the general welfare of the citizens overrides the individual's right to free speech.

Option 3 **Let the Espionage Act stand but overturn Schenck's conviction.**

For the reasons stated in **Option 2,** the government has the right to deny free speech when it endangers the country and the well-being of its citizens. Therefore, you should leave the Espionage Act alone.

The strong language of the First Amendment, however, requires that the government be extremely cautious about overriding the right to free speech. Thus, the Supreme Court should allow infringements on free speech only when the speech poses both a strong and immediate threat to the nation.

The *Schenck* case does not pose that kind of danger. The language of the leaflets is mild, reasonable, and restrained. Nowhere does it urge citizens to riot or take any unlawful actions. The leaflets do two things: 1) they urge draft inductees to use every legal means possible to resist the draft, and 2) they present the option that recruits use the Thirteenth Amendment as the basis for challenging the draft in court.

Public sentiment now strongly favors the government's decision to fight the war, so there is little chance that the arguments made in the leaflets will have much effect on those who read them. Even if the Socialists did persuade a majority of people to accept their point of view, this would pose no danger to the republic. Instead this would actually uphold democracy by indicating to the government that its action did not have the consent of the people. The government could then change its policy to reflect the will of the people either by relying on volunteer soldiers or by withdrawing from the war altogether.

THE DECISION IS YOURS.
WHICH OPTION DO YOU CHOOSE?

Option 1   **Declare the Espionage Act unconstitutional and free Schenck.**

Option 2   **Uphold Schenck's conviction.**

Option 3   **Let the Espionage Act stand but overturn Schenck's conviction.**

The 1919 Schenck *case forced Oliver Wendell Holmes (1841-1935) and eight other Supreme Court justices to decide how far the government can restrict speech during times of war.*

The Supreme Court chose *Option 2.*

Justice Oliver Wendell Holmes wrote the opinion for this decision, which was supported by all eight of the other justices. The decision was announced on March 3, 1919. Holmes established the precedent that the First Amendment did not grant people an absolute right to say whatever they please at any time. "The most stringent protection of free speech would not protect a man in falsely shouting fire in a theater, and causing a panic," said Holmes. The right of free speech ends, he maintained, when it infringes on other people's rights.

Having declared that there were times when the government could make laws restricting speech, the Court faced the sticky issue of determining exactly what speech was protected under the Constitution and what was not. Holmes admitted that there could be no solid dividing line between the two. "The character of every act," he said, "depends upon the circumstances."

To give local, state, and federal judges some sort of guideline to follow in cases such as *Schenck*, Holmes offered the "clear and present danger" standard. He did this in his belief that the courts should be very cautious in allowing governments to interfere with free speech. "[The] question in every case is whether the words used are in such circumstances and are of such a nature as to create a clear and present danger that they will bring about the substantive evils that Congress has a right to prevent," he said.

Another issue in this case was to decide whether the speech in Schenck's leaflets posed a clear and present danger to the country. In Holmes's view, the fact that the country was at war made all the difference. "We admit that in many places and in ordinary times the [defendant] in saying all that was said in the circular would have been within [his] constitutional rights," Holmes announced. In his view, however, this was not one of those times, and a draft induction line was not the place. Under the current circumstance, Schenck's leaflets endangered military recruitment and other national security interests.

The Court ruled that the leaflets were not protected under the First Amendment to the Constitution and thus upheld Schenck's conviction.

RESULT

Although the justices ruled unanimously in the *Schenck* case, they hardly settled the issue of what speech was protected by the First Amendment. The ruling established that the constitutional right to free speech had limits, but the majority of the court did not exercise the sort of caution that Holmes had envisioned in interfering with free speech.

In case after case following *Schenck*, the Supreme Court upheld the convictions of those prosecuted under both the Espionage Act and the even more restrictive Sedition Act of 1918, which made it illegal to say or write virtually anything critical of the government in times of war. The Court's stance made it dangerous for people even to discuss the war in their own homes for fear of saying something that would bring them arrest under the Sedition Act.

While the court used Holmes's *Schenck* opinion to justify these prosecutions, Holmes himself pulled back from the majority. Complaining that the court was not adhering to his strict test of a "clear and present danger," he began to argue more strongly in favor of free speech. Less than a year after the *Schenck* decision, in a case involving five Russian immigrants convicted of urging factory workers to strike, Holmes offered this stirring clarification of his views on free speech:

> But when men have realized that time has upset many fighting faiths, they may come to believe . . . that the best test of truth is the power of the thought to get itself accepted in the competition of the market and that truth is the only ground upon which their wishes safely can be carried out. That at any rate is the theory of our Constitution. . . . Only the emergency that makes it immediately dangerous to leave the correction of evil counsels to time warrants making any exception to the sweeping command, "Congress shall make no law . . . abridging the freedom of speech."

Over the course of the next several decades, the Supreme Court gradually adopted this cautious interpretation of this later decision concerning the government's right to interfere with free speech.

2

THE FLAG SALUTE
BOARD OF EDUCATION V.
BARNETTE
1943

In 1941, the West Virginia legislature amended state laws so that all schools were required to offer courses designed to promote patriotism and an appreciation of American ideals. Following this lead, on January 9, 1942, the West Virginia State Board of Education issued an order declaring that all public school authorities in the state must make saluting the U.S. flag "a regular part of the program of school activities." The order required all students to participate. Any child who did not honor the flag would be expelled, considered unlawfully absent, and could be sent to reformatories for juvenile delinquents. The state could also fine parents of these children $50 and sentence them to 30 days in jail.

This order posed a great problem for a religious group known as Jehovah's Witnesses. These people noted that the Book of Exodus in the Bible issued a commandment against "bowing down" to "any graven image, or any likeness of anything that is in heaven above, or that is in the earth beneath, or that is in the water under the earth." The Jehovah's Witnesses took these words seriously. In their view, the biblical command forbade them to salute a flag. Therefore, no matter how strong their loyalty to the United States, they refused to take part in the West Virginia flag salute.

As a result, several school districts expelled children who were Jehovah's Witnesses and threatened them with criminal proceedings. Three of the parents involved—

Children salute the United States flag at this camp in Comstock, Michigan. Many parents, however, feel that children should not be required to salute the flag in public school.

Walter Barnette, Paul Stull, and Lucy McClure—have brought suit in federal district court. They claim that West Virginia's flag salute rule is a violation of their religious freedom and their freedom of speech as guaranteed by the First Amendment to the Constitution.

A federal district court agreed with the Jehovah's Witnesses that West Virginia's flag salute law violated their religious freedom and issued an order preventing the law from being enforced. The West Virginia State Board of Education has appealed that decision to the Supreme Court.

LEGAL HISTORY

The First Amendment is at issue again, but this time the focus has shifted to the clause that says, "Congress shall make no law respecting an establishment of religion, or prohibiting the free exercise thereof." The authors of the Constitution had seen numerous examples of government intolerance toward religious beliefs. During the eighteenth century, many settlers whipped Quakers and Baptists and sometimes killed them because of their beliefs. Roman Catholics were denied the right to vote. All people in Virginia, regardless of their religious beliefs, were forced to give money to the Anglican church.

The founders of the U.S. government had included the First Amendment clause on religion to prevent the power of government from interfering with an individual's religious beliefs. As Thomas Jefferson stated in his Bill for Establishing Religious Freedom, adopted by the state of Virginia in 1786, religious freedom meant that no one

West Virginia public school officials expelled Marie (left) and Gathie Barnette because they would not salute the U.S. flag.

Thomas Jefferson (1743-1826), the third president of the United States, believed that all citizens should be guaranteed religious freedom.

would in any way "suffer on account of his religious beliefs" and that all people "shall be free to profess, and by argument maintain, their opinions in matters of religion."

As with the clause on free speech, the courts have held that the right to religious freedom is not absolute. There have been flag salute regulations in the United States since the state of Kansas initiated the practice in 1907. The issue of whether these rules are constitutional has come before the Supreme Court on four different occasions. The Court dismissed the first three cases on the grounds that they were matters of local law that did not concern the federal courts. This followed the Court's opinion that the freedoms stated in the Bill of Rights applied only to federal laws, not to state or local laws. Recent Supreme Court decisions, however, have said that the Fourteenth Amendment bars state and local government from infringing on any freedoms mentioned in the Bill of Rights.

The fourth case, which is almost identical to the one you are now considering, came before the Supreme Court only three years earlier. In the 1940 case of *Minersville School District v. Gobitis,* the children of a Jehovah's Witness family in Pennsylvania had refused to comply with a local school's regulation requiring a flag salute. Although many people believed that the Gobitas family (the last name was misspelled in the court records) were fine people and good citizens, the school expelled

Walter Gobitas and his children, William and Lillian, challenged mandatory flag saluting only three years before the Barnette *case, but the Court did not rule in their favor.*

the Gobitas children for their disobedience. The Gobitas family sued to discontinue the requirement of the salute for their children, saying that the rules violated their family's religious beliefs—beliefs that were protected by the First Amendment.

A federal district court in Philadelphia upheld the Gobitas family's complaint, but the Minersville School District appealed the case to a higher federal court. When they lost there as well, the school officials continued their appeal to the U.S. Supreme Court. In an 8-to-1 decision, the Court ruled in their favor, declaring that the school board had a legal right to require certain school programs and that "the flag salute is an allowable portion of a school program."

YOU ARE A JUSTICE ON THE U.S. SUPREME COURT.

You must consider the arguments and choose between the options presented.

Option 1 **Reverse the lower courts and hold to the** ***Gobitis*** **decision that supports the right of the West Virginia School Board.**

There is no reason for the Supreme Court to waste time considering the *Barnette* case, which is so similar to the *Gobitis* case that was decided just three years earlier. The purpose of the Supreme Court is to provide the final say in legal matters so that everyone knows what the laws are. The *Gobitis* case clearly established the law as it pertains to freedom of religion and freedom of expression versus flag salutes. In that case, the Supreme Court ruled that a school board has the right to require flag salutes in public schools regardless of how these might violate someone's personal views.

Considering the *Barnette* case and reversing the *Gobitis* decision so soon would make the Court the laughingstock of the legal system. If the laws of the land can be so easily twisted that they mean one thing now and exactly the opposite three years later, no one will have confidence that he or she is obeying the law. For the sake of a stable legal system, the Court should do nothing more than cite the precedent of *Gobitis* and apply it to all future cases. In this case, that means ruling in favor of the West Virginia School Board.

Besides the need for consistency, there is ample evidence that the Supreme Court's earlier decision was correct. In writing the *Gobitis* decision, Justice Felix Frankfurter put the matter clearly. "The ultimate foundation of a free society is the binding tie of cohesive sentiment," he said. "National unity is the basis of national security. . . . We live by symbols. The flag is the symbol of our national unity, transcending all internal differences, however large, within the framework of the Constitution."

As in the *Schenck* case, the *Barnette* case is taking place during a time of national crisis. The United States has recently gone to war against the powerful armies of Germany and Japan. Those countries have shown no qualms about conquering any nation they can defeat, and they have shown little mercy in their dealings with their defeated enemies. All Americans must pull together in this perilous struggle. As Justice Frankfurter said, the

With U.S. soldiers battling the Nazi armies of Adolf Hitler during World War II, many Americans felt it was more important than ever to show respect for the United States and its traditions.

government is well within its rights in these times to "encourage feelings of patriotism, though the measure might offend some." Respected organizations such as the American Legion have strongly backed West Virginia in its flag salute ruling.

You can sympathize with the plight of the Jehovah's Witnesses. But an individual's rights end when these rights infringe upon the rights of others, and that is what this case is about. As Justice Frankfurter explained, "the mere possession of religious beliefs does not relieve the citizen of public responsibility." The Constitution will defend a person's right to believe that all criminals must be put to death, but it will not protect someone who chooses to act on this belief from murder charges.

Some people have said that the flag salute order is needlessly restrictive and its penalties are too harsh. They wonder why the state simply can't excuse people such as

In the Gobitis *decision, Justice Felix Frankfurter (1882-1965) argued that saluting the flag was an important sign of patriotism.*

the Jehovah's Witnesses from participating in the flag salute. However, excusing them would weaken the unity of the nation and, in the words of the Supreme Court's *Gobitis* decision, "might cast doubts in the minds of the other children which would themselves weaken the effect of the exercise."

Option 2 **Uphold the lower courts in reversing the *Gobitis* decision. Rule in favor of Barnette and the Jehovah's Witnesses.**

Although the Supreme Court normally would not want to reverse a decision it made such a short time ago, this case is an exception. The *Gobitis* decision sparked a wave of indignation from legal experts, newspaper columnists, religious leaders, educators, and ordinary citizens around the country. Groups such as the American Bar Association and the American Civil Liberties Union are supporting the Jehovah's Witnesses in their legal action in this latest case. Even more importantly, three of the Supreme Court justices who voted to uphold the flag salute in *Gobitis* have publicly stated that they believe their decision in that case was incorrect.

Justice Harlan Stone, the only justice who voted against his colleagues in the *Gobitis* case, pointed out the hypocrisy of the flag salute law. This regulation tried to encourage patriotism and a love of American ideals by denying the very model of freedom for which the United States stood. Stone wondered what could be less supportive of American principles than the practice of forcing "these children to express a sentiment which, as they interpret it, they do not entertain, and which violates their deepest religious convictions."

A lower court echoed these arguments when it ruled in Barnette's favor in this case. This court said that the mandatory flag salute violated rights "which we regard as

Harlan Stone (1872-1946), the only justice to dissent from the majority opinion in the Gobitis *decision, thought forcing students to salute the flag was an act of oppression.*

among the most sacred of those protected by constitutional guaranties."

Recent events have shown how wrong Justice Frankfurter had been to suppose that you could promote national unity by denying individual freedoms. The *Gobitis* decision in 1940 touched off a flurry of violence and persecution against Jehovah's Witnesses throughout the country. Angry, self-proclaimed patriots took the Court's decision as a license to burn the Jehovah's Witnesses' kingdom halls where they worshiped, to assault these "unpatriotic" criminals, and to drive them out of their homes. Some communities passed laws banning the Jehovah's Witnesses' religion. By saying that patriotism was something that could be rammed down the throats of unwilling people, the Supreme Court achieved just the opposite of what Frankfurter had sought. Instead of encouraging national unity, the *Gobitis* decision of 1940 encouraged lawlessness, intolerance, and the worst kind of division between citizens.

THE DECISION IS YOURS.
WHICH OPTION DO YOU CHOOSE?

Option 1   Reverse the lower courts and hold to the *Gobitis* decision that supports the right of the West Virginia School Board.

Option 2   Uphold the lower courts in reversing the *Gobitis* decision. Rule in favor of Barnette and the Jehovah's Witnesses.

Robert Jackson, who wrote the majority opinion for Board of Education v. Barnette, *served for one year as the U.S. attorney general before his appointment to the Supreme Court in 1941.*

The Supreme Court chose *Option 2*.

Three justices who had supported the flag salute in the *Gobitis* case—Hugo Black, Frank Murphy, and William Douglas—changed their minds and adopted Harlan Stone's position. Two new justices, Wiley Rutledge and Robert Jackson, also agreed with Stone to form a 6-3 majority supporting the rights of the Jehovah's Witnesses. The majority did not simply try to modify the earlier *Gobitis* decision. Instead, they flatly declared that the *Gobitis* ruling had been a mistake.

Robert Jackson wrote the *Barnette* decision, which was announced, ironically, on Flag Day—June 14, 1943. Skewering Frankfurter's argument that society needed to encourage total support of a point of view, Jackson said

Appointed to the Supreme Court in 1943, Wiley Rutledge was the least experienced of all the justices who ruled on the Barnette *case, which said that requiring public school students to salute the flag was unconstitutional.*

that in a free society, the only way to guarantee that everyone is in complete agreement is to kill those who disagree with the majority. Obviously, the Constitution did not favor this.

To Frankfurter's claim that the flag was a "symbol of our national unity transcending all internal differences, however large, within the framework of the Constitution," Jackson pointed out that "a person gets from a symbol the meaning he puts into it." Justice Jackson observed that the Court could sustain the compulsory flag salute only by saying that "a Bill of Rights which guards the individual's right to speak his mind, left it open to public authorities to compel him to utter what is not in his mind."

That, said Jackson, was totally against everything the Constitution stood for. "If there is any fixed star in our constitutional constellation," he wrote, "it is that no official, high or petty, can prescribe what shall be orthodox in politics, nationalism, religion, or other matters of opinion, or force citizens to confess by word or act their faith therein. If there are any circumstances which permit an exception, they do not now occur to us."

Justices Black and Douglas added a written opinion in support of Jackson that said expressions of loyalty are meaningful only when they are freely given. "Words uttered under coercion are proof of loyalty to nothing but self-interest," they said. "Love of country must spring from willing hearts and free minds."

RESULT

By completely changing their minds within a three-year period, the Supreme Court justices made a radical break with tradition and the principle of following precedents. That they were willing to do so indicates the tremendous emotional hold the flag-saluting issue had on them and on the country. The immediate result of the ruling was that it prohibited state and local governments from requiring public flag salutes and pledges of allegiance.

This ruling, however, did not end the controversies over respect for the flag, nor the right of government to regulate religious actions. Nor has it decisively settled questions about an individual's right to be excused from statutes that violate his or her religious principles. Many people disagreed with the court's decision, and in many places flag salutes remained a regular part of the school routine. But because of the *Barnette* decision, communities were able to enforce these flag salutes only by the general agreement of those concerned and not by threat of punishment.

The Supreme Court's ruling, announced in the middle of one of the United States' most dangerous wars and when national interests were most likely to override individual rights, guaranteed that the Bill of Rights would retain a prominent place in the legal system of the United States.

3

SEPARATE BUT EQUAL
BROWN V.
BOARD OF EDUCATION
1954

The laws of the state of Kansas provide that any city with a population greater than 15,000 can choose to have either integrated elementary schools or separate-but-equal schools for black and white students. The city of Topeka has opted for racially separated schools.

The local chapter of the National Association for the Advancement of Colored People (NAACP) was concerned over this policy and, in 1950, developed a plan to challenge the dual school system of Topeka. By that autumn, the NAACP found 13 African-American parents who were willing to join in a lawsuit against the Topeka school board. Following the NAACP's suggestions, the parents tried to enroll their children in the white schools closest to each of their homes, but the children were denied enrollment because they were black. This gave the NAACP attorneys enough information to file suit on behalf of the 13 parents and their 20 children. The case, *Brown v. The Board of Education of Topeka*, was named after one of the plaintiffs in the case: Oliver Brown, who participated on behalf of his oldest daughter, Linda.

A federal court sympathized with the plaintiffs, agreeing that the segregation of the Topeka schools was not in the students' best interests. But the court also cited the 1896 case of *Plessy v. Ferguson* that declared the Constitution permitted separate-but-equal facilities for black and white citizens. The federal court ruled that the black and white schools in Topeka provided about the same level of education. Because of this, the city's practice of segregated schools did not violate the law, and Brown had no legal basis for complaint.

The attorneys appealed the case, and eventually *Brown v. The Board of Education of Topeka* has made its way to the Supreme Court of the United States. The Court grouped the case together with four other suits filed against segregated school districts in the District of Columbia, Delaware, South Carolina, and Virginia. All of these suits demand admission for black students into white schools, based on two claims: 1) the facilities at black schools are not as good as those at white schools, and therefore the black students are being denied the "equal protection of the laws" guaranteed by the Fourteenth Amendment, and 2) the very institution of segregated schools is a violation of black students' right to equal protection.

The Brown v. Board of Education *case was named for Oliver Brown, who—along with 12 other parents of Topeka, Kansas—joined in the suit to try to end school segregation.*

Like 19 other black students in 1950, Linda Brown was not allowed to register at one of Topeka's all-white public schools.

LEGAL HISTORY

The *Brown* case has its roots in the enslavement of blacks, which was legal in many parts of the United States until the time of the Civil War in the 1860s. The Thirteenth Amendment, adopted in 1865, abolished slavery. But discrimination against blacks continued in the years that followed. Virtually all states outside New England had laws segregating blacks from whites. The most common of these provided for segregated public schools.

During the years following the Civil War, the federal government took a number of steps to see that blacks were treated more fairly. The most important step was the passage of the Fourteenth Amendment, which was approved by the states in 1868. This amendment states in part, "No state shall make or enforce any law which shall abridge the privileges or immunities of citizens of the United States; nor shall any state deprive any person of life, liberty, or property, without due process of law, nor deny to any person within its jurisdiction the equal protection of the laws."

The amendment, however, proved to be of little practical value. State courts consistently ruled that the equal-protection guarantee of the Fourteenth Amendment did not apply to segregation laws. Near the end of the nineteenth century, almost 30 states continued to have laws requiring separate schools for blacks and whites.

The landmark 1896 case of *Plessy v. Ferguson* originated as a challenge to a Louisiana law that required separate railroad cars for black and white passengers. Critics of the law chose Homer Plessy as a particularly good example of the absurdity of segregation. By all appearances, Plessy was a white man; in fact, he was only one-eighth black. Nevertheless, railroad authorities had him arrested for refusing to leave the section reserved for whites.

Plessy's lawyers argued that this violated his rights under the Fourteenth Amendment. But, in an 8-to-1 decision, the Supreme Court disagreed. Louisiana, said the Court, had the right to segregate races traveling in railroad cars as long as the state provided equal facilities for both. Justice Henry Billings Brown based his decision on a "separate-but-equal" principle that had first been declared in the Massachusetts courts in 1850. According to Justice Brown, the Fourteenth Amendment guaranteed *equal* facilities but nothing more. He went on to declare that separation of the races was not only permitted by the Constitution but was also good policy. In

During the 1890s, Justice Henry Billings Brown helped to give legal backing to "separate-but-equal" practices, which led to the dispute over school desegregation more than 50 years later.

1899, the Supreme Court expanded the separate-but-equal laws to cover public schools specifically.

The *Plessy* decision paved the way for a flurry of "Jim Crow" laws designed to keep the races separate. (The name Jim Crow may have been derived from an old minstrel song.) State legislatures passed laws requiring segregated hotels, restaurants, theaters, restrooms, and drinking fountains. A Birmingham, Alabama, statute even made it illegal for black and white persons to play dominoes or checkers together.

In many cases, states have paid only lip service to the "equal" part of "separate but equal." Recognizing this, the courts occasionally have ruled against discrimination. The 1950 case of *Sweatt v. Painter* concerned a black Texan who wanted to attend a state law school. Texas

In southern states, drinking fountains, like schools, buses, and restaurants, were often segregated.

denied him entrance to the school. But to comply with the separate-but-equal law, the state hastily established a law school for blacks.

The Supreme Court ruled against Texas in this case and ordered the state to admit Sweatt to the white law school. In the Court's view, Texas's claim of equality between the white and the black law schools was laughable. As Chief Justice Fred Vinson wrote, "It is difficult to believe that one who had a free choice between these law schools would consider the question close." The school for whites had the advantages of experienced teachers, a solid curriculum, and influential alumni. Since the state could not offer these features in their black law school, Sweatt's right to equal treatment under the laws required Texas to admit him to the school for whites.

YOU ARE A JUSTICE ON THE U.S. SUPREME COURT.

You must weigh all the evidence and choose among the options provided.

Option 1 **Uphold the lower court's ruling in favor of the Topeka Board of Education's right to separate facilities.**

The Supreme Court has already ruled on this question. Its decision, establishing the separate-but-equal doctrine, has been effective for more than 50 years. You may agree with segregationists that "God Almighty drew the color line and it cannot be obliterated." Or you may find these attitudes disgusting. But either way, a judge does not make policy or impose her or his own views.

Legislators, not judges, have the task of making laws. As Justice Oliver Wendell Holmes was fond of pointing out, legislators have a constitutional right to make total fools of themselves. A democracy allows the voters to evaluate the performance of elected officials and vote out of office those who have not met the public's standards.

The Supreme Court's role is not to pass judgment on the wisdom of the laws—only to decide whether the laws are legal under the Constitution. Chief Justice William Howard Taft made this point when a case challenging the constitutionality of segregated state schools came before the Court in 1927. He wrote that the issue

William Howard Taft (1857-1930), who served as president of the United States from 1909 to 1913 and as chief justice from 1921 to 1930, was the only president ever appointed to the Supreme Court.

"has many times been decided [by the Supreme Court] to be within the power of the state legislatures to settle without the intervention of the federal courts."

Even more so than most state laws, statutes involving the education of students are matters for local officials. Even if the Supreme Court could do this practically—and it can't—it has no business acting as a board of education for the entire United States.

Furthermore, no legal basis exists for arguing that segregated schools deny the equal protection that the Fourteenth Amendment guarantees. After all, the members of the United States Congress who wrote the amendment saw nothing wrong with also enacting a law that segregated the schools in the District of Columbia. Many states, both in the North and the South, continued to operate segregated school systems even after they supported the Fourteenth Amendment.

***Option 2* Uphold the separate-but-equal principle of *Plessy v. Ferguson* but tighten the requirements of what is considered equal.**

This is a compromise solution for a difficult problem. On the one hand, the Supreme Court has established that separate-but-equal facilities are allowed under the Constitution. This point of law has been a part of the culture for nearly 60 years—it has shaped the way people have ordered their lives and their communities. The court's sudden overturning of that law would create all sorts of disruptions.

Furthermore, the separate-but-equal policy is obviously the will of a large segment of the population.

Currently, 17 states, including several outside the old Confederacy, have separate schools for blacks and whites.

On the other hand, even though the lower court that ruled on the Brown case upheld *Plessy*, that court noted that segregating schools harms black children. While on the surface many communities give the appearance that facilities are equal for both blacks and whites, most people know that white students get the better of the deal. Part of the reason for this inequality is that many segregated school systems have consistently spent much more money and given far more advantages to white schools than to black schools. In other words, the school systems are not strictly complying with the separate-but-equal order of the Court.

Blacks are far worse off than whites in this country, both economically and politically. Many sociologists believe that better education is the key that would allow blacks to gain social equality. Black people will never do so if they continue to receive an inferior education.

What can the Court do to promote true equality while not infringing on the segregation allowed by the Constitution? To be practical, the Court must support the separate-but-equal ruling of *Plessy* while at the same time tighten the rules against inequality, as it did in the *Sweatt* case. The court should demand an objective, comprehensive study of the facilities in Topeka, the other states named in the suits, and other locations as well. The Court should then spell out exactly what school districts must do to guarantee equal facilities in the eyes of the law. Those that fail to meet these standards will be forced to integrate their schools.

Option 3 Overturn *Plessy v. Ferguson* and order all school districts to integrate immediately.

"Separate but equal" has always been a ploy to keep blacks in a position of near-slavery that denies them meaningful roles in society. Arguing for the plaintiffs from four states and the city of Washington, D.C., Thurgood Marshall, head of the NAACP's legal defense fund, insists that "the rule of *Plessy v. Ferguson* was conceived in error and should be reversed" because even if all facilities for blacks and whites were identical, the very nature of segregation is unequal.

Justice John Marshall Harlan had been able to see this back in 1896 when he dissented from the Court's

In 1967, 13 years after Brown v. Board of Education, *Thurgood Marshall (1908-1993) became the first African American appointed to the U.S. Supreme Court.*

verdict in *Plessy*. That decision, said Harlan, did nothing less than "permit the seeds of race hatred to be planted under the seed of law."

Justice Harlan cut through the hypocrisy when he said that everyone knew that segregation laws were never intended to produce equality. After all, white people had designed these laws to exclude blacks. In 1896, Harlan said that these laws "proceed on the ground that colored citizens are so inferior and degraded that they cannot be allowed to sit in public coaches occupied by white citizens." As Harlan had predicted, the *Plessy* decision stamped blacks as inferior, with disastrous consequences for American justice. Following that decision, racial violence against blacks, including lynchings, increased.

The Fourteenth Amendment guarantees equal protection under the law for blacks. In the original congressional debate over the amendment, one of its supporters, Jacob Howard of Michigan, declared that the amendment "abolishes all class legislation in the states."

For proof that segregated institutions are unequal even when they offer equivalent facilities, you have only to listen to the testimony of experts. Several psychologists have testified before the Court that segregation has a harmful psychological effect on black children. Since legal separation of the races is seen as a sign of black inferiority, the separation automatically gives black children the sense that they are less important than whites.

The argument that the federal courts have no business deciding what is essentially a local issue is nonsense. Over the past 30 years, the Supreme Court has consistently held that the Fourteenth Amendment's guarantee of equal protection under the laws applies to all state and local laws.

Although the precedent of *Plessy v. Ferguson* has stood for more than 50 years, the decision is now clearly outdated. The ruling assumed the racist belief, which was common at the time, that whites were superior to blacks. Since that time, the United States has slowly risen above that kind of prejudice. The brutal tactics of Nazi Germany in the 1930s and 1940s brought out into the open the horrors of race discrimination.

Many white Americans came to realize that their own prejudice against blacks was the same type of bigotry as that of the Nazis in their persecution of Jewish people in Europe. In 1946, President Harry Truman established a national Committee on Civil Rights and called for an end to segregation laws. At about the same time, black athletes became accepted and popular members of previously whites-only sports teams.

This shows that the tide has changed. The Court must stop clinging to the relics of a bygone age. You must rule that the children in these cases be admitted to the white schools in their neighborhoods and order an immediate end to segregated schools.

Option 4 **Overturn *Plessy v. Ferguson* but allow segregated school districts to integrate gradually.**

Segregation has been a way of life for many communities, particularly in the South. Many people believe passionately that this way of life is best.

Any order demanding that segregated school districts immediately change their ways will provoke hostile resistance in some areas of the country. A backlash of angry whites could threaten the safety of any blacks who tried to assert their rights by enrolling in white schools and could create a national crisis by defying this ruling.

Also, a sudden change would create enormous difficulties for communities, school officials, and families. More than 2.5 million black students and 8.5 million white students presently are enrolled in racially segregated schools in 21 states. The task of immediately uprooting and rearranging all those students would be a nightmare.

Certainly, segregated schools are wrong, and you must overturn the separate-but-equal doctrine. But you should consider the effect of reversing *Plessy*. You should heed the advice of Justice Felix Frankfurter, who says that there is "nothing worse than for this Court to make an abstract declaration that segregation is bad and then have it evaded by tricks." Instead, you should be flexible. Rather than devise a huge scheme for desegregating all schools immediately, you should give local school officials the leeway to settle the matter themselves and ample time in which to complete the change.

THE DECISION IS YOURS.
WHICH OPTION DO YOU CHOOSE?

Option 1   Uphold the lower court's ruling in favor of the Topeka Board of Education's right to separate facilities.

Option 2   Uphold the separate-but-equal principle of *Plessy v. Ferguson* but tighten the requirements of what is considered equal.

Option 3   Overturn *Plessy v. Ferguson* and order all school districts to integrate immediately.

Option 4   Overturn *Plessy v. Ferguson* but allow segregated school districts to integrate gradually.

The Supreme Court chose *Option 4.*

On May 17, 1954, the Court ruled unanimously to overturn *Plessy v. Ferguson.* In his explanation of the decision, Chief Justice Earl Warren declined to sort out the complex issue of what may or may not have been intended by the authors of the Fourteenth Amendment almost a century earlier. The important thing to consider is what the Fourteenth Amendment means in modern times.

Warren noted the importance of education as a reason why the Court could not sit back and rely on *Plessy,* a half-century-old ruling. "Education is the very foundation of good citizenship," said Warren. "[It is] perhaps the most important function of state and local governments."

He then faced squarely the issue of legal segregation. "Separate educational facilities are inherently unequal," he said, because they foster a feeling of inferiority in blacks. Citing the evidence of "modern authorities," Warren wrote that the "segregation of white and colored children in public schools has a detrimental effect upon the colored child. The impact is greater when it has the sanction of law. We conclude that in the field of public education, the doctrine of separate but equal has no place."

The Court, however, did not order immediate integration of all schools. In fact, it delayed its decision on how segregated schools should be made to conform to the law. After hearing more arguments on this issue, the court issued a second opinion on May 31, 1955. The court's remedy did not apply immediate deadlines for desegregation. In an effort to defuse the fears of those who had lived under the separate-but-equal code all of

Chief Justice Earl Warren argued that by allowing segregated schools, the United States had neglected its responsibility to provide the best educational facilities possible for all of the nation's children—regardless of their race.

their lives, the opinion simply stated that officials must work "with all deliberate speed" to break down the official racial barriers.

RESULT

In declaring separate-but-equal laws unconstitutional, the Supreme Court provoked scathing criticism. Some legal scholars argued that the Court's action in breaking with legal tradition and dismissing previous court rulings was a "clear abuse of judicial power."

However, in *Cooper v. Aaron,* a case that came before the Court less than four years after *Brown,* the Supreme Court unanimously reaffirmed the *Brown* decision. The three justices who had joined the Supreme Court since the *Brown* decision declared that they agreed with the verdict.

Throughout the southeastern United States, state and local government officials denounced the *Brown* ruling and took official actions to fight or ignore it. More than 100 members of the United States Congress declared that the Court's ruling was "contrary to the Constitution."

The *Brown* decision triggered numerous outbreaks of violence and many attempts by local officials to disregard the ruling. The widespread outrage was an indication that the Court acted prudently in granting some leeway in its desegregation order. Had it ordered immediate desegregation, the Court could well have provoked even more hostility.

Some legal scholars argue that the Court's ruling created only chaos and confusion—that the problem of segregation would have solved itself more peaceably had the courts stayed out of it.

However, the fact that segregated school districts overwhelmingly took advantage of the Court's lenient time frame for desegregating weakens their case. Ten years after the *Brown* decision, less than two percent of black students in 11 states were attending previously all-white schools. Segregation in public places remained firmly in place in many parts of the South. Its dismantling began only after the 1965 Voting Act guaranteed blacks a political voice in those states. Had the Court

Desegregation turned dangerous in 1957 when President Dwight Eisenhower ordered federal troops to protect black students attending the newly integrated Little Rock Central High School.

waited for "normal channels" to take care of segregation, civil rights progress in the United States would likely have proceeded at a snail's pace.

As it was, a frustrated Supreme Court finally lost patience with the lack of progress. In 1965, the Court announced, "Delays in desegregating school systems are no longer tolerable." Since local authorities failed to solve the problem themselves, the federal courts began to exercise the powers given them under *Brown* to order more drastic remedies, such as busing and racial quotas for schools. These measures were frequently unpopular and hotly debated.

Despite the problems, complaints, and violence surrounding the *Brown* case, the decision is widely considered "one of the most humane acts in our history," one historian has said. The importance of the *Brown* decision was perhaps more symbolic than practical. By declaring an end to governmental support of segregation, the ruling gave an important boost to the civil rights movement that went on to develop during the 1960s. The decision held out the promise of equality for blacks and gave Congress the courage to enact laws that would help to fulfill those promises.

4

LAWYERS FOR THE POOR
GIDEON V. WAINWRIGHT
1963

C larence Earl Gideon, born in 1910, in Hannibal, Missouri, lived a dreary life on the far fringes of respectable society. Growing up in an unhappy family, he ran away from home at age 14. Desperately cold that winter, Gideon broke into a store in Missouri and stole some clothing. The police caught him, and a Missouri court sentenced him to three years in a reform school.

For most of his life, Gideon barely scraped by, never fitting in with any community. He wandered about the country, trying to hold on to a variety of short-term, low-paying jobs. When short of cash, Gideon turned to gambling and petty theft. His frequent brushes with the

Clarence Gideon, who was in trouble with the law much of his life, believed that people accused of crimes should have the right to free legal representation.

law left him with a record of four minor felony convictions, and he spent nearly 17 years in prison.

Loneliness also dogged Gideon throughout his life. After being married and divorced twice, he married a woman with three children and tried to settle down to a stable life in Panama City, Florida. He even became active in a local church. But tuberculosis and the pressures of providing for his growing family wore him down. While he was recovering from surgery to remove part of his lung, his wife left him and placed their children on public welfare. Hoping to earn enough to regain custody of the children, Gideon worked as an automobile mechanic, but he never managed to save enough money to support his children.

In the early morning hours of June 3, 1961, someone smashed a window of the Bay Harbor Poolroom, a tavern in Panama City. The burglar took a few bottles of beer and wine and some coins from the cigarette machine and the jukebox.

A witness named Henry Cook reported that he saw Clarence Gideon inside the pool hall very early that day. He said that he later saw Gideon leave with a bottle of wine. But Gideon insisted that he was innocent. He claimed that he worked part time at the tavern and had a key to the place. If he had wanted to sneak in, he could have done so without breaking a window. But Gideon's long record of petty thefts and his reputation as a gambler made Henry Cook's story easy to believe.

Gideon's case came to trial on August 4. When Judge Robert McCrary, Jr., asked Gideon if he was ready for the trial, Gideon said he was not because he had no lawyer. "Your Honor, I request this Court to appoint counsel to represent me in this trial."

Judge McCrary informed Gideon that he could not honor that request. Under Florida law, the court could provide a lawyer for a defendant only when that person was facing a possible death sentence.

Gideon then argued his case before the jury. He called eight witnesses to support his innocence. But the jury found him guilty of breaking and entering with intent to commit a felony. Because of Gideon's four previous convictions, the judge gave him the maximum sentence of five years in prison.

Gideon was convinced that the state had denied him his constitutional right to a free lawyer. In April 1962, he wrote a letter to the United States Supreme Court, asking them for justice. Gideon, who had read law books during his time in prison, followed all the formal rules of an appeal. His case has come before the Court's consideration.

You and the other justices on the Supreme Court have agreed to review his complaint. The case is known as *Gideon v. Wainwright*—Louie Wainwright being the director of Florida's Division of Corrections.

LEGAL HISTORY

Gideon based his appeal on the Fourteenth Amendment. He mistakenly thought the Supreme Court had ruled that, based on the Fourteenth Amendment's guarantee of due process, all states had to provide lawyers for those

Louie Wainwright (left) became director of Florida's prison system in 1959, when he replaced H.G. Cochran, Jr. (right).

charged with crimes who could not afford representation. But the Court had not done this.

The legal argument over the right to counsel actually has its roots in old English law. At the time that the United States won its independence from England, English courts did not allow felony defendants to have lawyers represent them. The founders of the United States believed that a person charged with a crime had a right to legal counsel. As a result, they adopted the Sixth Amendment, which says, "In all criminal prosecutions, the accused shall enjoy the right . . . to have the assistance of counsel for his defense."

Originally, the amendments in the Bill of Rights applied only to federal laws. States were free to make their own laws and were not bound by federal law. The due-process guaranteed to citizens was, historically, whatever legal procedures an individual state set up, as long as those procedures were fair.

The Fourteenth Amendment comes into play in the *Gideon* case because it specifically guarantees that the states will provide "due process" and "equal protection of the laws." In 1925, the Supreme Court first began to consider this amendment to mean that the right of free speech guaranteed under the U.S. Constitution applied to state and federal laws. A logical extension of this reasoning is that the right of counsel guaranteed by the Sixth Amendment also applies to state courts.

The question of whether the government must provide free lawyers for those defendants who could not afford them did not come before the Supreme Court until 1932. The case of *Powell v. Alabama* concerned the sensational trial of eight black teenagers accused of raping two white women. The very thought of this type of crime provoked passions bordering on hysteria among whites in the community where the trial was held.

The judge presiding over the case denied the defendants a lawyer until the day of the trial. The jury then convicted the black youths of rape. The defendants appealed their convictions on the grounds that they were denied the right to counsel.

The Supreme Court overturned the conviction. Noting the hostile atmosphere as well as the lack of preparation time, the Court ruled that the young men had been denied a fair hearing. The Supreme Court declared that having a lawyer in a serious criminal case was a fundamental right of all American citizens and that the due-process clause of the Fourteenth Amendment guaranteed this right in state as well as federal courts. The Court ruled that in order to guarantee this right, states had to provide lawyers to poor defendants on trial in state courts for crimes punishable by death.

Following this case, defendants in less serious cases asked for free lawyers. But the courts limited the scope of the *Powell* ruling so that states are only required to provide lawyers in special circumstances. In addition to cases involving a possible death penalty, these special circumstances included defendants who are uneducated or otherwise unable to defend themselves.

Two other precedents apply here. In the 1938 case of *Johnson v. Zerbst,* the Court ruled that the Sixth Amendment required that counsel be provided for all defendants in federal cases who were too poor to afford their own lawyer.

The case of *Betts v. Brady,* decided in 1942, involved a Maryland farm worker who was convicted of robbery. Unable to afford a lawyer, Smith Betts asked the Maryland court to provide one for him. Since his was not a capital case (one involving a possible death sentence), the judge refused. Betts appealed to the Supreme Court, which ruled against him. In a 6-3 decision, the Court refused to go beyond a narrow interpretation of *Powell v. Alabama.* It ruled that poor people had a right to court-appointed lawyers only in capital cases and under special circumstances.

Since that time, most states have extended the right to a court-appointed lawyer to include most, if not all, felony cases. Florida, however, is one of 13 states that provides lawyers only in capital punishment cases and in special circumstances.

YOU ARE A JUSTICE ON THE U.S. SUPREME COURT.

You must weigh all the evidence and choose among the options presented.

Option 1 **Strike down *Betts v. Brady* and uphold Gideon's appeal.**

In the twentieth century, a lawyer is an absolute necessity for obtaining a fair trial in an American court of law. Anyone who has ever stepped into a modern courtroom knows how quickly one can get lost and confused in the legal system without the aid of someone who knows how it operates. Legal jargon is virtually unintelligible to the average person, and few people understand all the points of law that apply to their case. Even someone like Clarence Gideon, who has a great deal of experience with the courts, was unable to mount much of a defense at his Florida trial.

Abe Fortas, who is arguing Gideon's case, insists that the aid of legal counsel is "indispensable" to a fair hearing. His reasoning is simple. The first thing that wealthy people do when charged with a crime is hire the best lawyer they can afford. They do this because they understand that the better the lawyer, the better the

In 1965, two years after representing Gideon, Abe Fortas was appointed to the Supreme Court— but stepped down from the high court under public pressure in 1969.

chance that the jury will find them not guilty. Poor people charged with the same crime are unable to afford lawyers and have nowhere near the same chance as the wealthy to avoid conviction.

The Fourteenth Amendment guarantees all citizens "due process" and "equal protection under the laws." What kind of equal protection is provided when wealthy people with lawyers have an overwhelmingly greater chance of winning their cases than poor people without lawyers? The only way to establish equal protection is to provide poor people with lawyers. Only then will they have the same chance as the wealthy to obtain justice from the courts. This right to an attorney is especially important in view of the fact that a large percentage of those charged with felonies are poor, uneducated people.

The *Betts v. Brady* decision, which denied the right to free counsel in many state criminal cases, does not establish a legal tradition or precedent. The decision in the *Betts* case was a mistake that actually strayed from the court's rule of law that had been established in earlier cases. *Powell v. Alabama*, for example, clarified that poor people charged with serious crimes in a hostile atmosphere needed a lawyer in order to obtain due process. *Betts v. Brady* turned that around and said that *only* those people who fell under the specific circumstances described by *Powell* had a right to a lawyer.

Furthermore, *Johnson v. Zerbst* established that poor people must be provided lawyers in order to ensure a fair trial in federal court. The *Betts* ruling somehow assumes that state courts are different. That simply is not logical. When the charges are equally serious, why does a person need a lawyer to get a fair trial in federal court but not in state court?

Most state governments are convinced that the right to a court-appointed lawyer is an idea whose time has come. Twenty-three states, which normally would be expected to support Florida's rights, have filed "friend-of-the-court" briefs urging that the right to counsel be made a constitutional requirement.

Florida is one of only a few holdouts that grants the right to a free lawyer only in capital cases and special circumstances. "Special circumstances" is the kind of vague language that makes for poor law because it provides no clear guidelines as to what *is* a special circumstance that guarantees the right to a lawyer. Without such guidelines, defendants cannot be certain exactly what their rights are.

Option 2 **Uphold** *Betts v. Brady* **and deny Gideon's appeal.**

The Sixth Amendment guarantees people the right to have an attorney. However, the authors of the Bill of Rights did not intend to force the government to provide and pay for that lawyer.

The Court has already spoken in cases of this sort. They have ruled that the right to court-appointed lawyers applies only to federal cases, not to state cases. States have the freedom to regulate their own procedures to provide due process. The only requirement that the federal courts have put upon state courts is to provide counsel for poor people in capital cases or special circumstances. The only way the Supreme Court could support Gideon's appeal is to overrule itself. For the stability of the country, the Court should be very careful about overruling itself on important cases.

Florida's assistant attorney general, Bruce Jacob, notes that the freedom to establish their own system of due process is a "historic right reserved to the states." A federal court ruling that restricted the right of states to govern themselves would be an unwelcome interference with states' rights.

"The states should not be straitjacketed," said Justice Owen Roberts in *Betts v. Brady*. Florida is well within its rights to set up its own judicial procedures as long as those procedures are fair. The state made every effort to provide Gideon with a fair trial. The judge and jury were impartial, Gideon had ample opportunity to plead his case and confront and cross-examine his accusers, and no special circumstances apply to his case. He is a man of average intelligence who is familiar with the court system, as evidenced by his ability to write his own appeal to the Supreme Court. Florida law does not entitle him to a court-appointed lawyer. Providing him one would be a case of special treatment, not justice.

Option 3 Uphold _Betts v. Brady_ but grant Gideon a new trial on the grounds that his is a "special circumstance."

Clarence Gideon's conviction is suspicious. The jury found him guilty on the evidence of one man who claims to have seen him come out of a pool hall in the early morning hours. Yet that "witness" did not report this supposed crime to the police; he gave his testimony only after being questioned by the police.

Gideon's defense was hopelessly inept. He may be familiar with the courts, but the man has only an eighth-grade education. You can hardly expect him to hold his own against the law-school graduates prosecuting his case. Abe Fortas, in reading the transcript of the trial, saw many occasions in which a qualified lawyer could have raised doubts about Gideon's guilt. Gideon, for example, made no objection to any evidence presented by the prosecution.

Gideon presents a strong argument for the idea that poor people need lawyers to get a fair trial. On the other hand, think of the burden you would impose on society by overruling _Betts_ and demanding free lawyers for all defendants in felony cases who are too poor to afford their own.

The state of Florida has more than 5,000 prisoners who were tried without lawyers to represent them. Many of these prisoners are hardened criminals. Overruling *Betts* would mean that Florida would have to release or retry all of these convicts. Furnishing free lawyers in all these cases would create an overwhelming demand for lawyers, tie up the courts for years, put convicted felons back on the streets, and place an enormous financial burden on the taxpayers.

The only practical solution for ensuring justice for Gideon—without endangering society—is to uphold Florida's law, based on the *Betts* decision, but grant Gideon a new trial because of "special circumstances."

THE DECISION IS YOURS.
WHICH OPTION DO YOU CHOOSE?

Option 1   **Strike down *Betts v. Brady* and uphold Gideon's appeal.**

Option 2   **Uphold *Betts v. Brady* and deny Gideon's appeal.**

Option 3   **Uphold *Betts v. Brady* but grant Gideon a new trial on the grounds that his is a "special circumstance."**

Justice Hugo Black, who had dissented from the majority in Betts v. Brady *in 1942, was still on the bench 21 years later when the Court heard* Gideon v. Wainwright, *a similar case about the rights to legal representation.*

The Supreme Court chose *Option 1*.

The Court's decision, announced on March 18, 1963, was unanimous. It reversed the *Betts* ruling and declared that having a lawyer was "fundamental and essential" to a fair trial in felony cases.

Justice Hugo Black, who had dissented in the *Betts* case, explained the Court's reasoning. He believed that the right to a court-appointed lawyer was necessary to ensure that every defendant stands equal before the law. He argued that "there can be no equal justice where the kind of trial a man gets depends on the amount of money he has." Denying lawyers to the poor amounted to putting people in jail just because they had no money, he said, and he insisted that the Constitution did not allow this.

In the *Gideon* decision, Black cited rulings such as *Powell v. Alabama* to show that the *Betts* ruling had been a mistake. He went on to say, "Not only these precedents but also reason and reflection require us to recognize that in our adversary system of criminal justice, any person hauled into court, who is too poor to hire a lawyer, cannot be assured a fair trial unless counsel is provided for him."

The right to a lawyer in criminal cases, said Black, was a necessity, not a luxury.

RESULT

The Supreme Court granted Clarence Gideon a new trial and appointed lawyer W. Fred Turner to represent him. Turner's tough questioning of the witness who claimed to have seen Gideon in the pool hall cast doubt on the prosecution's case. A jury acquitted Gideon of the charge after only an hour's deliberation. The warnings about the flood of criminals set loose by the *Gideon v. Wainwright* decision turned out to be partially accurate. Within a year of the court's ruling, the state of Florida released about 1,000 prison inmates who had been tried in court without the benefit of a lawyer. More than 500 additional convicts were brought back for retrial.

The *Gideon* decision did not accomplish everything that the justices hoped it would; it could not guarantee equal justice for all. The wealthy were still able to hire better lawyers and get a better chance of acquittal than poor people.

But the case still accomplished two important things. First, it solidly established the rights of the poor to court-appointed lawyers in criminal cases. Two months after the Supreme Court decided *Gideon*, the Florida legislature enacted a public-defender law, and other states followed suit. The policy became firmly established, as a wide range of legal experts praised the decision as long overdue.

Second, the case provided a stunning example that the American justice system makes every effort to treat all people fairly regardless of wealth or status. Even a down-and-out drifter like Clarence Gideon was able to get a hearing before the highest court in the nation.

5

CRIMINAL CONFESSIONS
MIRANDA V. ARIZONA
1966

I n the early morning hours of March 3, 1963, an 18-
year-old Phoenix, Arizona, woman was kidnapped and
raped on her way home from a movie theater. Ten days
later, police appeared at the home of Ernesto Miranda, a
23-year-old man with a lengthy police record, and took
him to the police station. Miranda stood in a line-up
with three other Hispanic men for the victim to identify.

The victim thought Miranda might have been her
assailant, but she could not positively identify him. The
police, however, told Miranda that she had. During
nearly two hours of questioning, at which time no lawyer
was present, Miranda confessed to the crime. He signed
a written confession and waiver stating that he had given
the confession voluntarily and with "full knowledge of
my legal rights."

In 1963, police arrested Ernesto Miranda for kidnapping and raping an 18-year-old woman in Phoenix, Arizona.

At his trial in an Arizona court, however, Miranda changed his story. He claimed that his confession was false and that, contrary to the waiver he had signed, no one had informed him of his rights prior to the confession. He asked that the confession be withdrawn as evidence in the case.

Ruling against Miranda, the trial judge allowed the prosecution to introduce the signed confession as evidence. A jury found Miranda guilty of kidnapping and rape, and the court sentenced him to two prison terms of 20 and 30 years each.

While in prison, Miranda appealed his case to the Arizona Supreme Court. He argued that his constitutional rights had been violated because he was not informed of his right to speak to a lawyer before the interrogation, and he was not aware that what he told police could be used against him at his trial.

The Arizona Supreme Court upheld Miranda's conviction. Miranda has now appealed to the United States Supreme Court.

LEGAL HISTORY

This case presents a conflict between police officers, who are trying to protect citizens, and the rights of individuals accused of a crime. Guilt in a crime is often difficult to prove, and throughout much of history authorities have used force, even torture, to persuade suspects to confess to crimes.

The founders of the United States were keenly aware that innocent people will confess to crimes they have not committed in order to escape severe pain and suffering. They believed that their new country could not assure citizens of justice if authorities could force suspects to admit guilt. To prevent this, the founders adopted a clause in the Fifth Amendment that states that "No person . . . shall be compelled in any criminal case to be a witness against himself, nor be deprived of life, liberty, or property, without due process of law."

Miranda claims that the police violated this amendment. The defendant also claims that the authorities ignored his Sixth Amendment right to "the assistance of counsel for his defense."

There are some conflicting precedents in this case. In 1934, the Arizona Supreme Court stated that informing a criminal suspect of his or her rights was "the better and safer course," but the court also declared that the law did not require police to do so.

In 1936, however, a particularly graphic example of police brutality prompted the United States Supreme Court to consider the rights of the accused. *Brown v. Mississippi* involved three black men accused of murder. Interrogators hanged one of the men from a tree and whipped him until he confessed. They severely whipped the others with a leather strap until they, too, signed confessions.

On the basis of those confessions, a Mississippi court found the men guilty and sentenced them to death. The U.S. Supreme Court, however, overruled the verdict on the grounds that the accused were denied due process. In the words of Chief Justice Charles Evans Hughes, "It would be difficult to conceive of methods more revolting to the sense of justice than those taken to procure the confessions." The Court observed that any confession that is not given voluntarily cannot be considered reliable evidence in a court of law.

The most recent Supreme Court statement about rights of the accused occurred in the case of *Escobedo v. Illinois.* On January 20, 1960, police arrested Danny Escobedo in connection with the murder of his brother-in-law. They handcuffed the suspect and questioned him for about four hours at police headquarters. Throughout the interrogation, Escobedo repeatedly asked to speak to his lawyer. His lawyer arrived at the station and over a period of three or four hours repeatedly asked to speak to his client. Police refused to allow the two to meet.

Two years after the Supreme Court heard his case, Danny Escobedo sits in a Chicago police station— charged with burglarizing a hot-dog stand.

Police eventually got Escobedo to admit that he had participated in the crime. At his trial, Escobedo argued that he was tricked into providing incriminating evidence against himself. But, primarily on the basis of Escobedo's confession, the Illinois court convicted Escobedo and sentenced him to life in prison. The Illinois Supreme Court upheld the verdict, but Escobedo continued his appeal to the U.S. Supreme Court.

In 1964, the Supreme Court ruled that the police had violated Escobedo's rights and that they could not use his confession as evidence. Writing for the Court, Justice Arthur Goldberg said that because the police had failed to advise Escobedo of his right to remain silent and had denied him the opportunity to consult with his lawyer, "the accused has been denied 'the assistance of counsel' in violation of the Sixth Amendment."

In the majority opinion of the Escobedo *case, Justice Arthur Goldberg, who served on the Supreme Court from 1962 to 1965, wrote that criminal suspects must be allowed to consult with their attorneys.*

YOU ARE A JUSTICE
ON THE U.S. SUPREME COURT.

You must weigh the evidence and decide among the available options.

Option 1 **Reverse the Arizona court. Rule that Miranda's confession cannot be presented as evidence and require police to inform defendants of their constitutional rights prior to interrogation.**

The Fifth Amendment clearly prohibits police from "compelling" people to testify against themselves. The Sixth Amendment clearly guarantees the accused the right to consult with a lawyer. The police did not inform Ernesto Miranda of either of these rights prior to the questioning that produced his confession. Without the benefit of counsel from an attorney, Miranda had signed a vague waiver that said he was aware of his rights. But in the absence of any explanation of those rights, that waiver was nothing more than a trick.

Unless you strongly enforce the Fifth and Sixth amendments, you will expose citizens to brutal intimidation and physical harm at the hands of police. You will be responsible for destroying the Constitution and creating a system in which the police can arrest innocent citizens and force them to confess to crimes they did not commit.

Most police officers are decent, conscientious professionals who routinely respect other people's rights. Therefore, requiring them to observe the rights of the accused does not hinder them in any way. Tightening the rules on confessions merely prevents bad cops from getting out of control. As Justice Goldberg argued in the *Escobedo* decision, "If the exercise of constitutional rights will thwart the effectiveness of a system of law enforcement, then there is something very wrong with that system."

Stronger guarantees of the rights of the accused are necessary to help clarify for police what evidence is permissible and what is not. Even good police walk a fuzzy line between skillful interrogation and threats of intimidation. If the police inform the accused of their rights before questioning, then no doubts will exist about whether any statements suspects make can be used as evidence.

Many people argue that police have a tough enough job to do and that tightening the rules on confessions will make their job impossible. Since the 1940s, FBI agents have made a practice of informing suspects of their right to remain silent and to have a lawyer present. This practice has not hurt their effectiveness.

In any case, a judge cannot allow people to violate the law just because those laws make their jobs more difficult. Former Justice Louis Brandeis argued in a previous case that the government cannot bend laws and constitutional rights even if doing so will make life more convenient. "If the government becomes a lawbreaker," said Brandeis, "it breeds contempt for the law; it invites every man to become a law unto himself; it invites anarchy."

During his 23 years as a Supreme Court justice, Louis Brandeis (1856-1941), who had been called "The People's Lawyer" as an attorney, consistently supported the rights of individuals.

***Option 2* Uphold the Arizona court. Permit Miranda's confession to be used as evidence and do not require warnings.**

By Arizona law, the police do not need to inform a suspect of the right to remain silent. Furthermore, the constitutional protections of the right to remain silent and the right to a lawyer pertain to a trial, not to the questioning of a suspect.

The police have a difficult job trying to protect the public from all kinds of vicious individuals. In order to do their job, they need to be able to extract the truth from untruthful people. Criminals usually do not play by nice, polite rules. What is wrong with police officers using a little pressure and some clever techniques to trick them into revealing the truth? After all, the truth is the important thing. If the police go too far in their techniques or if jury members think the confession might have been forced, a jury can easily throw out the confession at the trial.

Forcing the police to observe all kinds of niceties makes getting to the truth harder for them. By putting the burden on the police, you would give criminals an advantage in their fight against the law. All these red-tape requirements of informing people about rights will make confessions almost impossible to obtain. That will mean fewer arrests, fewer criminals convicted, and more criminals walking the streets. With the way violent crime is increasing, this course of action would be disastrous.

You need not be so concerned about the rights of criminals. What about the rights of the victims of these criminals? What about the ordinary citizen's right to protection from criminals? Aren't these rights worth at least as much protection as the rights of criminal suspects? How can society possibly function if law and order are sacrificed for the sake of the rights of a few questionable characters?

The *Escobedo* decision offers no firm basis for upholding Miranda's rights. Only five of the nine justices voted in favor of that decision. In a dissenting opinion, Justice Potter Stewart warned that the Court's ruling "frustrates the vital interests of society in preserving the legitimate and proper functions of honest and purposeful police investigations."

As to the specifics of the *Miranda* case, the police did nothing to intimidate Miranda or force him to confess. He freely volunteered the information. Miranda was a convicted criminal who had gone through the police interrogation scene many times and understood the process. He signed a waiver claiming full knowledge of his rights. In view of that, his claim that he was not aware of his rights rings hollow.

Miranda's complaint that the police had denied him the right to consult with a lawyer is just more legal maneuvering to save his skin. The man never requested a lawyer, so how can he complain about being denied the right to consult with one?

Option 3 **Reverse the Arizona court. Throw out Miranda's confession, but do not require warnings.**

For the reasons cited in **Option 2,** there is no reason to shackle the police with further requirements for protecting the rights of the accused. The present safeguards are adequate.

The *Miranda* case, however, presents a situation in which the police *did* overstep their legal boundaries. The officers used dishonest methods to force a confession. They made Miranda believe that the victim had positively identified him and that his conviction was assured. They threatened, in Miranda's words, to "throw the book at me" if he did not confess, and they offered to drop a robbery charge if he did.

According to Miranda, the officers hinted that a medical problem had caused him to act the way he did and that they could get help for him. They led him to believe that since he was as good as convicted, the best thing for him to do was to confess so that the Arizona court would be more lenient in sentencing him. Scared and worn down from lack of sleep, Miranda gave in.

Under such shady circumstances, you cannot consider Miranda's confession voluntary or reliable. You should overturn the previous verdict and bar the use of the confession as evidence in any retrial of the case.

THE DECISION IS YOURS.
WHICH OPTION DO YOU CHOOSE?

Option 1   Reverse the Arizona court. Rule that Miranda's confession cannot be presented as evidence and require police to inform defendants of their constitutional rights prior to interrogation.

Option 2   Uphold the Arizona court. Permit Miranda's confession to be used as evidence and do not require warnings.

Option 3   Reverse the Arizona court. Throw out Miranda's confession, but do not require warnings.

*Justice John M. Harlan, whose grandfather had also
served on the high court, recognized that Supreme
Court decisions do not always reflect popular opinion.*

The Supreme Court selected *Option 1*.

As in the *Escobedo* case, the Court was badly split. The decision, announced on June 13, 1966, won the support of only five of the nine justices.

Chief Justice Earl Warren, who wrote the majority decision for the Court, had a special interest in this case. As a district attorney in California early in his law career, Warren had been a hard-nosed prosecutor who boasted one of the highest conviction rates in the state for cases that he tried. But he admitted to being cautious not to trample on the rights of the accused.

Warren was keenly aware of the power the police hold in an interrogation room. He described how police officers use patience, determination, and tricks to "undermine the will to resist." The popular practice of isolating a suspect for relentless questioning, said Warren, "is at odds with one of our nation's most cherished principles— that the individual may not be compelled to incriminate himself."

Warren went on to say, "Unless adequate protective devices are employed to dispel" the intimidating atmosphere of police interrogation, then "no statement obtained from the defendant can truly be said to be the product of his free choice."

Regarding the *Miranda* case, Warren said, "It is clear that Miranda was not in any way apprised of his right to consult with an attorney, nor was his right not to be compelled to incriminate himself effectively protected in any other manner." Following the precedent of *Escobedo*,

Warren declared, "Without these warnings the statements were inadmissible."

As a former district attorney, Warren understood the temptation of police to bend or evade rules protecting the rights of the accused. So that no one could misunderstand exactly what the law allowed in questioning suspects, Warren came up with clear guidelines. Prior to interrogations, police had to inform suspects of four things: 1) their right to remain silent, 2) that anything they said could be used against them in court, 3) their right to the presence of an attorney, and 4) that if they could not afford a lawyer, the court would appoint one for them prior to questioning.

RESULT

The *Miranda* decision sparked a storm of outrage from dissenting justices, police, and irate citizens. Justice Byron White said that the decision set up an "impenetrable barrier to any interrogation" and asked how any meaningful police work could take place under these restrictions. The decision, said White, was "neither compelled nor even strongly suggested by the language of the Fifth Amendment" and was "at odds with American and English legal history."

Justice John M. Harlan denounced the decision as "poor constitutional law," not justified by any clause of the Constitution nor any Supreme Court precedent. The effect of the ruling, he said was "to negate all pressures . . . to discourage any confession at all." He believed that by exaggerating the evils of police questioning, Warren had issued a ruling that was dangerous to society.

Many police officers criticized *Miranda* as an unreasonable interference with their duties. Likewise, many citizens criticized the ruling as an example of judges being "soft" on crime and coddling criminals. People feared the prospect of hardened criminals being set free on technicalities, even when their guilt was obvious.

Arkansas Senator John McClellan blamed the soaring violent crime rate in the United States during the late 1960s on the *Miranda* decision. Richard Nixon denounced the ruling and, using a law-and-order theme as a keystone of his presidential candidacy in 1968, directed considerable criticism at the Supreme Court. Public anger over *Miranda* played a significant role in helping Nixon win a narrow victory over Hubert Humphrey. In the decades following *Miranda*, some Supreme Court decisions softened the hard-and-fast rules set by Chief Justice Warren.

However, the courts have upheld the basic concept of the *Miranda* ruling. The so-called *Miranda* warning has become a routine part of police work. Not only have police learned to accept it, but many law enforcement authorities have come to believe that the warning helps them to do a better job of ensuring that the evidence they collect will stand up in court.

As for Ernesto Miranda, the Supreme Court decision overturned his conviction. But it did not set him loose on the streets as Warren's critics had feared. Without using the confession as evidence, the authorities retried the case, and a jury found Miranda guilty of the

Criticizing the Miranda decision and running a staunch law-and-order campaign may have helped Richard Nixon (1913-1994) win the 1968 election for president.

The nine members of the Supreme Court who heard the Miranda case (from left to right): Tom C. Clark, Byron White, Hugo Black, William J. Brennan, Jr., Earl Warren, Potter Stewart, William O. Douglas, Abe Fortas, and John M. Harlan.

charges. The court sentenced him to the same prison term that the judge had handed down in the previous trial. Miranda was paroled in 1972. Four years later, he was stabbed to death in a fight in a Phoenix bar.

The legal resolution of the case provided a model for Chief Justice Warren's vision of equity. It confirmed his belief that the police could effectively do their jobs without infringing on what Warren viewed as the fundamental rights of all citizens.

6

ABORTION
ROE V. WADE
1973

In August 1969, Norma McCorvey told police that she had been a victim of a violent crime. In police headquarters, McCorvey, who worked in a traveling carnival, described what she said happened late one night when she was walking back to her motel outside Augusta, Georgia: Three men followed her, taunting and jeering. After McCorvey angrily spoke back to the men, they raped and beat McCorvey, who eventually fell unconscious.

When the local police openly doubted her story, McCorvey returned to her home state of Texas. The divorced McCorvey had no place to live. A friend helped out by letting McCorvey stay in her trailer. It was there that McCorvey discovered she was pregnant. But she did not want the baby—which she has said was the product of rape. She could not even care for her five-year-old daughter, who was living with McCorvey's mother. In fact, Norma McCorvey could barely afford to buy enough food for herself.

McCorvey discovered that she could not obtain a legal abortion in Texas because Texas law prohibited abortions except to save the life of the mother. In her words, "no legitimate doctor in Texas would touch me." McCorvey considered flying to California, where state law permitted abortion. The cost of the trip, however, was far more than she could afford. She finally found a Texas doctor of questionable reputation who would perform an abortion, but his prices were outrageously high. Anguishing over her situation, McCorvey saw no choice but to go through with the pregnancy.

A lawyer friend took pity on McCorvey and introduced her to two lawyers who were particularly concerned with women's rights. Encouraged by the lawyers, she challenged the constitutionality of the Texas law forbidding abortion.

In order to protect her identity, the suit referred to her only as "Jane Roe." The case became known as *Roe v. Wade*, in reference to Henry Wade, a prosecuting attorney in Dallas County, where the case originated.

The baby was born in June 1970, and McCorvey immediately gave the child up for adoption. Although it was too late for McCorvey to have an abortion, that month the U.S. district court in Dallas ruled in favor of her. Citing the Ninth Amendment, the court declared the

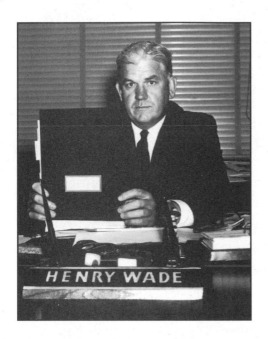

Years before Roe v. Wade, *Dallas County district attorney Henry Wade, pictured here in 1964, investigated the criminal activity of Jack Ruby, who had murdered President John F. Kennedy's alleged assassin, Lee Harvey Oswald.*

Texas law to be an unconstitutional imposition on individual rights. Texas has now appealed *Roe v. Wade* to the U. S. Supreme Court.

LEGAL HISTORY

Throughout the centuries, English common law usually did not consider abortion a crime. The United States followed that tradition in its early years. Before 1821, the United States had no laws restricting abortion. However, in the mid-nineteenth century the nation's doctors led an anti-abortion movement, whose primary purpose was to protect mothers from unsafe practices and incompetent practitioners. In 1854, the state of Texas adopted a law outlawing abortion except to save the mother's life. By

1910, every other state except Kentucky had made abortion a felony, with most granting an exception only when the pregnancy endangered the mother's life.

The pendulum began to swing back in the 1950s. Ironically, doctors generally favored loosening the restrictive laws. By the late 1960s, almost one-third of the states had begun to permit abortion in a wide variety of situations, including rape, incest, abnormalities of the fetus, and endangerment to the mother's health. Four states eliminated all criminal penalties for abortions in the early months of pregnancy. Roe is challenging the Texas statute that has remained on the books in its original form since 1854.

The federal court in Dallas cited the Ninth Amendment of the Bill of Rights as the basis for overturning the Texas law. This amendment contains only the subjective statement that "the enumeration in the Constitution, of certain rights, shall not be construed to deny or disparage others retained by the people." In other words, citizens' rights are not limited to those that the Constitution specifically spells out. The court construed the right to abortion as one of these unmentioned rights. The Fourteenth Amendment then made the Ninth Amendment apply to state and federal laws. The district court said that the state *could* override an individual's right to abortion under certain circumstances. But the court concluded that Texas had not shown that it had a "compelling interest" in interfering with this right.

Roe's lawyers are also referring to the Supreme Court's 1965 ruling in the case of *Griswold v. Connecticut.* This case came about when Estelle Griswold of Planned

Parenthood became frustrated with the unwillingness of Connecticut legislators to change a state law barring the use of contraceptives. In defiance of the law, she set up a birth control clinic in New Haven, where she distributed contraceptives.

A Connecticut court convicted Griswold of violating the law, but the Supreme Court threw out her conviction. On a 7-to-2 vote, the Court ruled that the Ninth Amendment guaranteed a "right of privacy" and that the Connecticut law violated that constitutional right.

State governments often cite the Tenth Amendment as clear evidence of their right to pass their own laws. This amendment says, "The powers not delegated to the United States by the Constitution, nor prohibited by it to the states, are reserved to the states respectively, or to the people."

YOU ARE A JUSTICE
ON THE U.S. SUPREME COURT.

You must weigh all the evidence and then choose among the options available.

Option 1 **Uphold the lower court decision. Declare the Texas law unconstitutional and assert a woman's right to abortion.**

You should uphold the lower court's decision, declare the Texas law unconstitutional and assert a woman's right to abortion. You should strike down the Texas law for legal, historical, moral, social, and health reasons. The legal support for a woman's right to abortion comes from the *Griswold* decision that established privacy as a fundamental right protected by the Constitution. This decision was a correct interpretation of the Ninth Amendment, which guarantees unlisted rights to the people, and of the Fourteenth Amendment, which protects individual liberties from the powers of state and federal government.

A woman's decision whether to have children is clearly a private matter that falls under this protection. This is not a case of a woman's rights versus the rights of the fetus. No court in the United States has ever recognized the fetus as a person. Therefore, this case is strictly a matter between the constitutional rights of the woman and the rights of the state. To override the individual's rights, the government would have to demonstrate that the state has a compelling interest in the case. Norma McCorvey's lawyer, Sarah Weddington, argues that what a woman does with her body does not threaten or otherwise affect the state in any way. Concerns for the mother's health

Sarah Weddington, only five years out of law school when she argued for abortion rights in front of the Supreme Court, remained a prominent attorney in the years following Roe v. Wade.

prompted original abortion laws, but modern medical advances have eliminated this concern. Abortion is now a simple and safe procedure when performed by qualified physicians.

The Texas abortion law is morally wrong. It forces women who are emotionally or financially unable to cope with parenting to bear children. By doing so, the law contributes to the tragedy of hungry, neglected, and abused children in society. Furthermore, because it causes hardship only for the poor and disadvantaged, the law violates equal protection provisions of the Constitution. Wealthy people can afford to travel to locations where abortion is legal, but the poor can't. Over the past few years, hundreds of Texas women flew to New York for abortions.

Socially, the Texas law is a relic of a different age. The state of Texas adopted the law at a time when society did not recognize women as worthy of equal protection under the law. A group of men, with no knowledge or concern for how pregnancy can completely disrupt a woman's life, voted for and passed the law. This is a different era. In March of last year, many U.S. politicians backed the Equal Rights Amendment, an indication that the country is finally willing to treat women fairly. Revocation of the Texas abortion law is simply another long overdue recognition of women's rights.

The argument that a fetus has the same rights as a mother is illogical. Even many abortion opponents are willing to allow abortion if it is needed to save the life of the mother. That means the country is virtually unanimous in saying the mother is worth more than the fetus.

In addition, the Texas law provides no punishment for a woman who performs an abortion on herself, only for those who perform abortions on others. The state can hardly argue that abortion is murder if it does not punish a woman who destroys her own fetus.

If the state has any interest at all in the abortion issue, it should be a medical interest. Yet the Texas statute is a case of government interference with medical practice. The law shows no respect for the professional judgment of physicians and encourages unsafe, illegal abortions among those too poor to afford legal ones. Since 1962, more than 5,000 American women died in unregulated abortions. These women would probably be alive today if restrictions such as those in the Texas law were removed.

***Option 2* Uphold the lower court decision that declares the Texas law unconstitutional, but restrict the right to abortion in the later months of pregnancy.**

While allowing you to accept many of the arguments in favor of a woman's right to abortion, this option recognizes that the issue is enormously complex—that there is no magic dividing line between what is fully human and what is potentially human. *Option 2* accomplishes a balancing act by following the example of medical experts.

Physicians commonly divide a pregnancy into three trimesters of about three months each. In the first trimester, the fetus is poorly developed and a woman can easily be pregnant without realizing it. During this time, the rights of the mother far outweigh the responsibility to the fetus, and so the right of privacy should guarantee a legal abortion in the first trimester. During the third trimester, the fetus is often capable of surviving outside the womb. The state should give special protection to a fetus so close to birth, so capable of independent life. You should prohibit abortions in this stage. The second trimester is the gray area. Rather than trying to play God and setting up specific statutes, the state should leave abortion decisions at this time to professional physicians and their patients.

Option 3 Reverse the lower court. Uphold the Texas law restricting abortion to only those cases in which the mother's life is threatened.

The time has come for the courts to stand up and recognize that the fetus is human. Life begins at the moment of conception. Within a few weeks of conception, a fetus develops many recognizable characteristics of a human. Moreover, advances in modern medicine have made possible the survival of babies well before they reach full term. A civilized, moral society should renounce once and for all the barbaric custom of killing its young. Surely the right of an innocent baby to live is more important than an adult's right to privacy.

Killing another human is murder. And killing an unborn human is just as much murder as the killing of any other human. The act of abortion is especially cruel because the victims are helpless and dependent on the mother for their care.

As to the argument that abortion should be a woman's choice, most women have a large degree of choice in whether or not they will get pregnant. Birth control methods are available. Once a child is conceived inside the mother, her responsibility to that child takes priority over any desire not to be inconvenienced by the pregnancy. Killing an unborn child is a highly inappropriate method of birth control, to put the matter mildly.

Even if you personally reject this argument, the state of Texas has every right to pass and enforce its own laws in this area. The Constitution, through the Tenth Amendment, guarantees states broad power to decide what kind of legislation should be enacted to protect the health and welfare of the public. Regardless of what you think of the Texas law, it was legally adopted by a legislature elected by the people of that state.

The *Griswold* decision was wrong in allowing abortion-rights supporters to hide behind a supposed Constitutional "right to privacy." As Justice Potter Stewart pointed out in his dissent in the *Griswold* case, no

Potter Stewart, who served on the Supreme Court from 1958 to 1981, firmly believed that justices should not infer rights and guarantees that are not clearly stated in the Constitution.

such right is mentioned anywhere in the Constitution or in any of the amendments.

Texas assistant attorney general Jay Floyd makes the point that the "freedom over one's body . . . is not absolute." The courts have approved many laws that restrict what we can do to our bodies. For instance, there are laws that prohibit people from putting certain drugs into their bodies. There are certain bodily functions that you cannot perform in public places. Stepping in to regulate a practice that generates such intense religious and ethical concerns is well within the rights of Texas.

Option 4 Uphold the lower court decision that declares the Texas law unconstitutional, but restrict the right to abortion only to cases of rape or incest.

This option allows you to accept many of the arguments in support of a state's right to outlaw abortion. But, like **Option 2,** this option is a compromise. While upholding the sanctity of life and protecting unborn children, **Option 4** recognizes that abortion is, on rare occasions, the best solution in a bad situation. The idea that a woman should be forced to carry a child that comes as a result of an assault is repugnant. By requiring a woman to do this, the Texas law places an unconstitutional hardship on the woman.

The fact that Norma McCorvey (alias Jane Roe) has not challenged this law on the basis of rape, which in any case was not proved in a court of law, makes this decision harder to justify on legal grounds. Yet the principle of freeing women from rape-induced pregnancies is strong enough that it demands a statement from the Court.

THE DECISION IS YOURS.
WHICH OPTION DO YOU CHOOSE?

Option 1   Uphold the lower court decision.
Declare the Texas law unconstitutional
and assert a woman's right to abortion.

Option 2   Uphold the lower court decision that
declares the Texas law unconstitutional,
but restrict the right to abortion in the
later months of pregnancy.

Option 3   Reverse the lower court. Uphold the
Texas law restricting abortion to only
those cases in which the mother's life is
threatened.

Option 4   Uphold the lower court decision that
declares the Texas law unconstitutional,
but restrict the right to abortion only to
cases of rape or incest.

Chief Justice Warren Burger, who served on the Supreme Court from 1969 to 1986, and the eight other justices who heard Roe v. Wade, *had a difficult time making a ruling on this controversial case.*

The Supreme Court chose *Option 2*.

Just as there was no clear consensus in American society as to how the abortion issue must be resolved, the Supreme Court had difficulty coming to an agreement on this case. Chief Justice Warren Burger said that "at the close of the discussion of the case there were literally not enough columns to mark up an accurate reflection of the voting."

Seven of the nine justices finally came to an agreement in *Roe v. Wade*, and they announced the result on January 22, 1973. Justice Harry Blackmun took on the task of drafting the reasoning behind the decision to strike down the Texas abortion law. Blackmun started off by recognizing the "deep and seemingly absolute convictions that the subject inspires."

After reviewing the history of abortion law, Blackmun maintained that precedents such as the *Griswold* case established that the Fourth, Ninth, and Fourteenth amendments to the Constitution protect a person's right to personal privacy. The right to terminate a pregnancy, Blackmun said, falls within this right of privacy.

This right is not absolute. But to deny this right, the state must demonstrate that the government has a compelling interest to do so. The state, said Blackmun, could not argue that this right to privacy interferes with a fetus's right to life because the Constitution does not recognize a fetus as a person. Blackmun, who was experienced in legal matters relating to medicine, did not get into the argument over when life began. But he disagreed with Texas's assertion that human life begins at conception and

Harry Blackmun, who served on the Supreme Court from 1970 to 1994, believed that the U.S. Constitution's right-to-privacy guarantee included the right to have an abortion during the early months of pregnancy.

that, therefore, the fetus is a person with protected rights. That was merely "one theory of life" that the state could not impose on all citizens. Blackmun was especially disturbed that this action interfered with the professional authority of physicians in determining what was best for their patients.

Blackmun, however, saw that the closer a fetus came to birth, the greater the responsibility the state had to protect that life. At some point, he conceded, this responsibility to protect life overrides a woman's right to privacy.

Blackmun used the medical approach of dividing a pregnancy into three trimesters. He said that in the first three months of pregnancy, a woman's right to privacy prevailed and the government could not interfere with that right. During the second trimester, the state could regulate abortions to protect the mother's health. In the

Byron White, who served on the Supreme Court from 1962 to 1993, was one of two justices who argued in 1973 that the high court had no business making a decision on abortion since the issue was not addressed in the Constitution.

third trimester, the state could intervene on behalf of the fetus and prohibit abortions.

Justices Byron White and William Rehnquist dissented from the majority of the Court. Neither found any evidence that the Constitution provided for a right of privacy, much less the right to abortion. They argued that the people, through their elected state legislatures, should decide abortion issues. Justice White criticized the decision as "an exercise of raw judicial power."

RESULT

Roe v. Wade triggered a negative public reaction similar to the reaction to the *Brown v. Board of Education* desegregation case. Some religious groups firmly opposing abortion spearheaded much of that opposition. Justice Blackmun was swamped with letters condemning his decision. A Roman Catholic cardinal from Philadelphia spoke for many when he said, "It is hard to think of any decision in the two hundred years of our history which has had more disastrous implications for our stability as a civilized society."

Nearly 20 years after Roe v. Wade, *Norma McCorvey speaks to reporters about the issue of abortion.*

Shock and outrage over the rulings helped fuel a growing and increasingly militant anti-abortion movement in the United States. However, a growing public sentiment in favor of a woman's choice in abortion countered the anti-abortion movement. Polls consistently showed a strong majority of American citizens favoring a woman's right to abortion, at least in certain circumstances. As far as influencing the country's attitudes on abortion, *Roe v. Wade* did little other than to intensify an already explosive political issue.

But the Supreme Court is supposed to decide cases according to legal principles, not by the strength of public opinion. While the *Roe v. Wade* decision has the support of many legal experts, it has also drawn an unusual amount of criticism as to its legal correctness. Critics blasted the decision as more radical than anything the Warren Court had ever done. Many legal experts agreed with Justice White's complaint that the justices were taking over the law-making role that properly belonged to elected officials in Congress and state legislators. Conservatives, especially, argued that the Court played fast and loose with the words of the Constitution to declare a "right to privacy" that simply did not exist. They complained that Blackmun did not base his abortion opinion on any specific provision of the Constitution, but rather on his own ideas of what the Constitution *should* say.

The criticism, however, did not prevent *Roe v. Wade* from exerting both an immediate and a lasting effect on the country. The ruling immediately struck down many state laws that prohibited abortions. The Court ruling has

In a handful of rulings following Roe v. Wade, *the Supreme Court continued to define abortion law in the United States, while demonstrators— on both sides of the issue—have tried to influence the Court's decisions.*

remained in force despite criticism and the opposition of presidents Richard Nixon, Ronald Reagan, and George Bush, all of whom were in office since the Court announced the decision. Furthermore, the courts have maintained the constitutional right to privacy declared in *Griswold*.

By using the pseudonym "Jane Roe," Norma McCorvey had protected her identity during the controversial case. Years afterward, McCorvey publicly disclosed her true identity and agreed to interviews by the press. She admitted that she had not been raped in 1969 and that for four months she had dated the father of the child she gave up for adoption.

In a 1993 interview, Norma McCorvey told a reporter that she would like to find out what happened to the child that she put up for adoption more than 20 years earlier.

7

REVERSE DISCRIMINATION
THE UNIVERSITY OF CALIFORNIA V. BAKKE
1978

A llan Bakke worked hard to secure a solid job as an aerospace engineer for a NASA research center in Palo Alto, California. But he could not suppress his desire to become a doctor. While working his regular job, this husband and father of three took on a nearly full-time course load to prepare for medical school. He also worked late hours as a volunteer in a hospital emergency room.

In 1973, Bakke felt he was ready to tackle medical school. He feared that his age, 33, might work against him. Yet he had a solid record as an undergraduate student at the University of Minnesota and as a graduate student at Stanford University. He also performed well on the Medical College Admissions Test. With solid credentials and letters of recommendation in hand, Bakke applied to 12 medical schools.

Bakke's dreams came to a crashing halt, however, when all 12 schools rejected him. He was especially upset when he discovered that one of the schools that rejected him, the University of California at Davis, had a special admissions program for minorities. Of the 100 openings for new students, the school reserved 16 for "economically and educationally disadvantaged minority applicants." Bakke found that his grades and test scores were far higher than those of students admitted under the special policy.

Bakke wrote to the Davis admissions committee, complaining that he was the victim of illegal discrimination. He believed that the university had denied him entrance simply because he was white. When the school still refused to admit him, Bakke brought a suit against the school in a California court. He argued that Davis's policy violated his rights guaranteed under the Fourteenth Amendment and the 1964 Civil Rights Act.

The California court ruled that the Davis admissions program discriminated on the basis of race, a violation of the law. The court ordered Davis to change the policy and to reconsider Bakke's application. The ruling satisfied neither the school, which wanted its admissions program to remain intact, nor Bakke, who wanted the court to order Davis to admit him.

The case went on to the California Supreme Court in September 1976. That court ruled that Davis's affirmative-action admissions program violated the Fourteenth Amendment to the Constitution, and it ordered the school to admit Bakke, who is now enrolled there. The University of California has appealed to the U.S. Supreme Court to reverse the ruling in this case, *Regents of the University of California v. Bakke.*

LEGAL HISTORY

After the Civil War, the United States ratified several amendments that were designed to end slavery and grant equal rights to black Americans. Those amendments were not effective, however, thanks to decisions such as the *Plessy v. Ferguson* segregation ruling in 1896. By the mid-twentieth century, black Americans still suffered discrimination and lagged far behind whites in education, political representation, income, and professional jobs. Medical schools, which were almost exclusively white, were a glaring example of the vast gulf of opportunity that still separated blacks and whites in the United States.

After a tense period of civil rights conflict in the early 1960s, Congress passed the Civil Rights Act of 1964, which prohibited discrimination in all public accommodations and made it illegal for employers to discriminate on the basis of race, color, religion, sex, or national origin. Basically, the act put teeth into the Fourteenth Amendment's guarantee of equal protection under the law for all citizens. The Supreme Court upheld the Civil Rights Act, confirming that Congress had the power to create such a law. But the economic gaps between blacks and whites caused by decades of discrimination would not disappear overnight. In 1965, President Lyndon Johnson issued executive action calling for universities and employers to take active steps to create more job opportunities for minorities and women. This type of policy became known as "affirmative action."

When the University of California at Davis opened its medical school in 1968, it found the lingering effects of past discrimination. Minorities made up only three percent of its first medical school class. Determined to include more minorities in its classes, the school adopted the affirmative-action program in effect at the time of Bakke's application.

The Supreme Court has ducked the issue of whether affirmative-action programs are legal ever since they were established. In 1973, the Court was asked to consider the case of *DeFunis v. Odegaard*. Marco DeFunis had

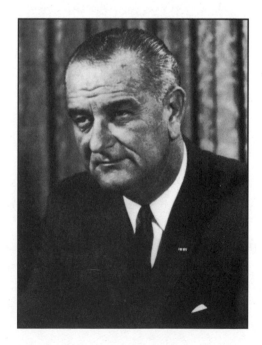

During more than five years in office, President Lyndon Johnson (1908-1973) became known as a strong supporter of the civil rights movement and programs to end discrimination.

Five years before Bakke, *the Supreme Court decided not to consider the case of Marco DeFunis (right), who claimed he had been a victim of reverse discrimination.*

failed to gain acceptance to the University of Washington law school, a school that used affirmative action to benefit minority applicants.

A Washington court accepted DeFunis's claim of racial bias and ordered him admitted to law school. The Washington Supreme Court reversed that decision and upheld the school's affirmative-action program. The Supreme Court, however, allowed him to stay in law school while his appeal was pending. DeFunis, who was already enrolled in his final semester of school, appealed to the U.S. Supreme Court. At that point, the Court decided there was no reason to hear the case because by then DeFunis was going to graduate no matter what the Court decided. Bakke, on the other hand, is still enrolled at Davis and doesn't expect to graduate for a few more years, so the Court had no reason to postpone hearing the case and considering this issue of reverse discrimination.

YOU ARE A JUSTICE
ON THE U.S. SUPREME COURT.

You must weigh all the arguments and choose from among the alternatives.

Option 1 **Uphold the California Supreme Court's decision admitting Bakke. Declare affirmative-action programs unconstitutional.**

The case is a clear instance of the type of racial discrimination prohibited by both the Civil Rights Act of 1964 and the Fourteenth Amendment's provision of equal protection under the law. Discrimination is discrimination, whether it is practiced against blacks or whites. As Bakke wrote in a letter to the chairman of the Davis admissions committee, "I realize that the rationale for these quotas is that they attempt to atone for past racial discrimination, but insisting on a new racial bias in favor of minorities is not a just situation." In fact, the policy simply subjects whites to the same type of injustice that blacks once received, the type of injustice that the Civil Rights Act of 1964 was written to end. Even Justice William O. Douglas, a champion of minority rights, wrote of the *DeFunis* case, "Whatever his race, [DeFunis] had a constitutional right to have his application considered on its individual merits in a racially neutral manner."

The United States can achieve equal protection of the laws only when people stop evaluating others on the basis of their skin color or sex or national origin. No excuse exists for considering race when choosing among applicants for employment or education.

Despite their noble intentions, affirmative-action programs of all kinds are harmful. Not only do they discriminate against whites, but they degrade minorities. Granting special consideration to minorities promotes the view that minorities are inferior, that they cannot compete honestly against whites. These programs cheapen the accomplishments of those minority individuals who *do* successfully compete against whites.

These programs are also harmful to society. As Bakke says, "Applicants chosen to be our doctors should be those presenting the best qualifications." Who wants to put their life in the hands of someone who is only marginally qualified and got into medical school because of a special admissions program? You cannot justify affirmative-action programs on the grounds that the state has a compelling interest in promoting racial harmony that overrides an individual's rights. These programs actually harm race relations by causing whites to resent minorities who get favorable treatment at their expense.

Option 2 **Reverse the California Supreme Court's decision admitting Bakke. Uphold the constitutionality of Davis's affirmative-action program.**

Many legal experts argue that affirmative action is simply a policy to help correct obvious wrongs of the past and to prevent future racial discrimination. It is naive to think that the United States can instantly grant equality after hundreds of years of slavery and discrimination simply by declaring that everyone now has an equal shot at competing in society.

Whites used illegal and unethical means to put blacks down and gain the advantages they presently enjoy. Now that whites have every advantage, they declare the competition to be equal and open. In fact, the competition is rigged against blacks. It is like whites running the first 50 yards of a 100-yard race while minorities stand shackled at the starting line. Suddenly the shackles are taken off and the race is declared free and open to everyone. How fair is the competition when the whites already have a huge head start?

The government has a compelling interest in making up for the injustices of the past so that the competition is more fair. As the Washington Supreme Court said in

Because blacks—who were once brought to the United States as slaves—and other minorities have been mistreated since the early years of the United States, many people now believe that affirmative-action programs are a reasonable way to make up for past injustices.

the *DeFunis* case, "The shortage of minority attorneys—and, consequently, minority prosecutors, judges, and public officials—constitutes an undeniably compelling state interest." An increasing number of black legal experts would help minorities to gain more faith in the legal system. Greater involvement of minorities in all highly skilled professions would help to erase racial stereotypes, break down barriers that exist between races, and provide role models for minority youngsters.

The medical school situation in the United States is riddled with terrible inequities that the government, in the interests of equal protection for its citizens, has a right to address. In 1967, only seven percent of the medical students in the United States were black (735 of 10,000), which is only half the percentage of blacks in the U.S. population. When you consider that most black medical students attend one of two medical schools, the low percentage of blacks at most schools is a disgrace.

The admissions policy at the University of California at Davis was made for a good cause; it was not designed to deny rights or discriminate against anyone. It is a serious effort to overcome some of the effects of the past and advance toward the goal of a more equitable society. The school's program of setting aside 16 out of 100 spots for minorities is hardly out of line in a state where more than one out of four residents is a minority. While the policy may not be perfect, you should give universities some leeway to experiment with ways of addressing social problems.

The Davis policy has attracted an impressive list of supporters. The American Bar Association, the

Unlike racial discrimination in the past, the quota system at the University of California at Davis medical school was designed to help minorities, not hurt them.

Association of American Medical Colleges, the National Council of Churches, the United Auto Workers, and others have filed briefs with the Court backing the university on this issue.

Option 3 Uphold the California Supreme Court's decision admitting Bakke but allow other types of affirmative-action programs.

As the arguments in **Option 2** suggest, you can make a strong case for some affirmative-action programs. You should leave public institutions free to correct past injustices, especially if those injustices linger despite all efforts to root them out. Deep-seated injustice calls for drastic measures. For example, normally the federal government tries hard to stay out of the business of creating plans to desegregate school districts. But when many school districts refused to comply with federal desegregation laws, the courts took over to enforce the laws of equal protection. You could make the case that whenever public institutions and programs fail to extinguish the smoldering embers of discrimination, the state has a compelling interest in affirmative action as a means of enforcing equal protection under the law.

The Davis medical school, however, came into existence relatively recently and has no such past history of discrimination. Also, universities do not violate the law when they express a preference for a certain type of student. For example, they are within their rights in favoring students with excellent academic records. They also routinely grant admission and scholarship preference to students for reasons that have nothing to do with academic performance. For instance, they actively recruit football players, even those who show little classroom ability. Schools also use a variety of criteria, such as leadership ability and personal recommendations, to ensure they get students who will be assets to their school.

Universities, then, would be well within their rights to seek minority students to establish the kind of racial diversity they desire. They could consider minority status as a favorable quality, alongside other favorable qualities such as grades, leadership ability, citizenship, and athletic talent. The Davis plan, however, does not merely consider minority status as a desirable quality; instead it has set up a rigid racial quota system.

By setting aside a specific number of openings for people of one race and then automatically denying other people those openings for no reason other than race, quotas cause senseless divisions that can tear a society apart. Even the Davis admissions people confess that Allan Bakke is better qualified to enter their school than many of those who got in ahead of him. But the inflexible nature of their plan excludes Bakke in violation of his civil rights.

These factors show that, while affirmative-action programs can be good and within the law, the Davis program is neither.

Option 4 **Uphold the California Supreme Court's decision admitting Bakke but decline to rule on affirmative-action programs in general.**

The Davis admissions policy is a discriminatory quota system that violates the Civil Rights Act of 1964. It should be outlawed for the reasons provided in **Option 1** and **Option 3**. A wise judge, however, sticks to the facts of the case and does not speculate on cases that do not come directly before him or her. The only decision that needs to be rendered here is whether the University of California at Davis violated Allan Bakke's civil rights. There is no reason to make a blanket decision on whether *all* affirmative-action programs are legal or illegal.

THE DECISION IS YOURS.
WHICH OPTION DO YOU CHOOSE?

Option 1   Uphold the California Supreme Court's decision admitting Bakke. Declare affirmative-action programs unconstitutional.

Option 2   Reverse the California Supreme Court's decision admitting Bakke. Uphold the constitutionality of Davis's affirmative-action program.

Option 3   Uphold the California Supreme Court's decision admitting Bakke but allow other types of affirmative-action programs.

Option 4   Uphold the California Supreme Court's decision admitting Bakke but decline to rule on affirmative-action programs in general.

The Supreme Court decided on *Option 3*.

The decision, which was handed down on June 28, 1978, was one of the most bizarre in Supreme Court history. Only one justice, Lewis Powell, actually voted for the decision adopted by the Court. Four justices voted to uphold affirmative-action programs, including Davis's *(Option 2)*. Four justices decided that Davis's admissions program violated Bakke's civil rights. But they refrained from ruling on affirmative-action programs in general *(Option 4)*. Only Lewis Powell chose **Option 3**. But his opinion prevailed because he provided the fifth vote that declared Davis's admissions program illegal and also the fifth vote that upheld the legality of affirmative-action programs in general.

Justice John Paul Stevens cited the Civil Rights Act of 1964 in explaining the decision against Davis. "Race cannot be the basis of excluding anyone from participation in a federally funded program," he wrote. (Public universities, such as the University of California, receive financial support from federal tax dollars.)

In arguing for affirmative-action programs, Justice William Brennan declared that such a program was legal when "it acts not to demean or insult any group, but to remedy disadvantages cast on minorities by past racial prejudice."

Powell was left to tie together both ends of the deeply divided Court. He wrote that racial classification was allowable under the Constitution as long as "race or ethnic background is simply one element—to be weighed fairly against other elements—in the selection process."

Justice Lewis Powell, who served on the Court from 1972 to 1988, helped to decide whether racial quotas were constitutional.

Justices John Paul Stevens (top) and William Brennan came to different conclusions about affirmative action in the Bakke case, confirming that even the nation's top legal experts can disagree.

He argued that schools had a right to take race into account in admissions because "the nation's future depends upon leaders trained through wide exposure to the ideas and mores of students as diverse as this nation of many peoples."

But Powell added that any program that took race into account had to be flexible enough to protect the rights of all individuals. The quota system set up by the University of California clearly violated the civil rights of Allan Bakke and others like him. He went on to declare that "when a state's distribution of benefits or imposition of burdens hinges on ancestry or the color of a person's skin or ancestry, that individual is entitled to a demonstration that the challenged classification is necessary to promote a substantial state interest."

The Davis admissions program, said Powell, did not demonstrate a substantial state interest. The desire to right the past wrongs of discrimination was noble, he argued, but was legally impractical. The present generation could not possibly reach back into history and remedy all the injustices of the past. The courts would not know where to start or end such a process.

RESULT

After five years of anxious waiting, 38-year-old Allan Bakke was admitted to medical school. He received his degree in 1982 and took up practice as an anesthesiologist.

As far as long-term effects on the nation, the fractured decision established no solid basis for future decisions about claims of reverse discrimination. The

In 1982, four years after the Bakke *decision, Allan Bakke receives his medical degree from the University of California at Davis.*

decision plainly outlawed admissions programs based on quotas. At the same time, it offered legal support for affirmative-action programs in general. Educators guessed that almost all affirmative-action admission programs in the country would hold up under the court's guidelines, so long as they did not use a quota system. The very next year, the Court strengthened its stand by permitting employers to set up affirmative-action programs as well.

Yet the split vote on *Bakke,* and the fact that Justice Powell could not persuade any of his fellow justices to agree with both ends of his "majority" decision, created a cloud of uncertainty over the issues. The Court left a great deal of room for future justices to decide the legality of efforts to achieve racial diversity and justice through affirmative-action programs.

8

THE RIGHT TO DIE
CRUZAN V. MISSOURI
1990

On January 11, 1983, 25-year-old Nancy Beth Cruzan lost control of her automobile on a road in Jasper County, Missouri. The injuries she suffered in the crash deprived her brain of oxygen for at least 12 minutes and left her brain dead. She now lies in what doctors call a "persistent vegetative state." She lives only because she is fed through tubes. Doctors hold no hope that she will ever improve.

Ten months after the accident, Nancy's parents, Lester and Joyce Cruzan, asked hospital personnel to remove the feeding tubes so that their daughter could be allowed to die. The state hospital that treated Nancy, however, refused to do so without permission from the

At a 1989 press conference, Lester and Joyce Cruzan speak to reporters about the medical condition of their daughter, Nancy.

courts. The Cruzans then sued the Missouri State Department of Health and asked a state trial court to grant permission to remove the life-support tubes.

Agreeing with the Cruzans, the court ruled that, under both state and federal constitutions, Nancy had the right to refuse life-sustaining measures. As she was incapable of exercising her right, her parents could exercise it for her. The health department appealed the ruling to the Missouri State Supreme Court. This court ruled in favor of the state and said that in life-or-death situations, Missouri law demanded convincing and reliable evidence of a person's wish to refuse treatment. Without such proof, no person, not even a parent, could presume to make that choice. This requirement held even though the patient was brain dead and in no way capable of making a decision for herself. The Cruzans have appealed this ruling to the United States Supreme Court.

LEGAL HISTORY

This is a situation in which advances in technology have changed the world dramatically since the time the Constitution was written. Modern medicine can now use artificial devices to keep people alive long past the point when they have any interaction with the world or any desire to remain alive.

The laws of the United States clearly prevent one person from killing another. But is the act of removing artificial life support really murder or is it simply allowing natural death to take place? The framers of the Constitution could not have anticipated such a dilemma.

For that reason, any constitutional questions on this issue are extremely difficult to answer.

Until recently, legal questions about the right to refuse treatment rarely surfaced. When they did, the questions usually had to do with parents forbidding medical treatment for their children because of their religious beliefs. In these instances, the courts have said the interests of the state in preserving a child's life override the parents' right to religious practices, no matter how strongly held their religious beliefs might be.

An actual "right-to-die" case has not previously come before the Supreme Court. However, the Court has issued some rulings that touch on matters presented in this case. About 100 years ago, the Supreme Court declared in the case of *Union Pacific Railway Co. v. Botsford*, "No right is held more sacred . . . than the right of every individual to the possession and control of his own person, free from all restraint or interference of others, unless by clear and unquestionable authority of law."

The federal court case that comes closest to probing the issues in the Cruzan case never advanced as far as the U.S. Supreme Court. The case involved Karen Quinlan, who lapsed into a coma in April 1975 and stopped breathing twice for about 15 minutes. Although her brain could still perform some functions, Quinlan remained in a persistent vegetative state and required an artificial respirator to keep her alive. She could not interact with the outside world in any way, and doctors had no hope that she would ever do so.

Seeing his daughter shrivel into an emaciated, almost unrecognizable shell of her former self, Joseph

In 1975, Joseph Quinlan argued that he should be able to take his daughter Karen (right) off life support, but the case did not go to the U.S. Supreme Court.

Quinlan asked a New Jersey court to declare him guardian for his daughter. He stated that his intent in gaining this power was to authorize the removal of all life-supporting equipment so his daughter could die naturally. When the lower court refused to grant this permission, Joseph Quinlan appealed to the New Jersey Supreme Court. He produced a statement from his bishop that said, "[The] decision of Joseph Quinlan to request the discontinuance of this treatment is, according to the teachings of the Catholic Church, a morally correct decision."

In 1976, the New Jersey Supreme Court ruled in favor of Joseph Quinlan. Citing the 1965 *Griswold v. State of Connecticut* case, the court said that Karen was entitled to relief from her life-sustaining treatment under her right of privacy. The court said that it could overrule this right, as well as Quinlan's right to act according to his religious beliefs, if these beliefs conflicted with compelling interests of the state. But the court saw no reason why the state had a compelling interest in keeping alive someone in a vegetative state. That still left the matter of whether Joseph Quinlan could make the "right-to-die" decision for Karen. The court decided that "Karen's right of privacy may be asserted on her behalf by her guardian under the peculiar circumstance provided."

Bouvia v. Superior Court, a more recent case, wrestled with the matter of a suffering, terribly disabled person's right to relieve the agony of living. Like the Quinlan case, this did not come before the U.S. Supreme Court. But a lower court judge decided the case in 1986 by saying, "The right to die is an integral part of our right to control our own destinies so long as the rights of others are not affected."

Lester and Joyce Cruzan face reporters after the Supreme Court hears arguments in the Cruzan *case.*

YOU ARE A JUSTICE ON THE U.S. SUPREME COURT.

You must weigh the evidence and decide among the choices available.

Option 1 **Reverse the Missouri court's decision. Grant the Cruzans' request to allow Nancy to die.**

The Missouri Supreme Court has made a cruel decision that serves no purpose other than to continue the suffering of the Cruzan family. The state of Missouri has nothing to gain from keeping Nancy Cruzan clinically alive when she is technically brain dead. In fact, given that Missouri is currently spending more than $130,000 per year simply to see that an otherwise lifeless body keeps breathing, the state's interests would be better served by taking Nancy off the life-support system.

The state is relying on an outdated concept of death. The world has changed. The medical community's ability to keep vital bodily functions continuing long after natural death would otherwise occur has upset and degraded the process of dying. Although many of these procedures are called "life supporting," they actually are "death prolonging." Many people dependent on life support systems are not experiencing any quality of human life.

The Missouri court's outdated stance is causing the Cruzans needless suffering. Nancy is gone; the family will never again be able to interact with her. Judge Lynn Compton declared in the *Bouvia* case, "If there is a time when we ought to be able to get the government off our backs, it is when we face death—either by choice or otherwise."

Yet the Missouri court is butting into this profoundly personal moment, so much so that it will not even permit the parents the dignity of allowing their daughter to die. The decision involved here may be painful, but it is one that only the family can make. Previous court decisions indicate that the courts recognize a person's right to refuse treatment. The Quinlan case has established that parents can assert the rights of their children in such tragic circumstances. Denying the right of the parents to make this decision for their children undermines the importance of the family in society.

The American people understand the problems that modern life-supporting technology has presented concerning the right to die with dignity. Recent polls have shown that about 80 percent of Americans now believe that there is nothing wrong with removing machines that keep the permanently vegetative humans alive.

Option 2 Uphold the Missouri court's decision to deny the Cruzans' request due to lack of clear evidence as to Nancy's wishes.

While the courts have determined that people have a right to refuse medical treatment, this case presents a more difficult problem. Nancy Cruzan is in no condition to make a decision to refuse treatment. In such a case, the question is, does anyone else have the right to refuse it for her?

The state of Missouri has adopted a law specifically to deal with this situation. The law says that in order for medical personnel to withhold treatment, there must be clear and reliable evidence of the patient's wish to refuse medical treatment. That is a logical and humane solution to the problem. It guards against the possibility of parents and others pulling the plug too soon on a person whom they, for various reasons, may not want to see live.

The Missouri law also releases parents and other family members from the awful burden of making a life-or-death decision that they may later regret. In times of sudden tragedy, shocked and grieving family members are in a poor frame of mind to make rational, intelligent decisions. The state has a compelling interest in protecting patients from the consequences of ill-advised decisions that would kill them.

Furthermore, whether you agree with the Missouri law or not, it *is* the law. It has come about through the legitimate legal processes set up by the people of that state. Since the law violates no specific constitutional right, the Court has no business interfering with the legislative process. The Supreme Court of the United States should stand aside and respect the right of each state to govern itself.

Option 3 **Uphold the Missouri court's principle of requiring clear and reliable evidence, but reverse its ruling in the *Cruzan* case.**

For all the reasons cited in **Option 2,** the Court should respect the Missouri law that requires clear evidence of a patient's wishes before allowing anyone, parents included, to make medical life-or-death decisions for them. But in this case, the Cruzans meet that requirement.

First, one of Nancy's friends testified in the Missouri court that Nancy had expressed her wishes for just such a situation. According to this friend, Nancy had once told her that she would not want to live if she could not have a fairly normal life.

Second, the lower courts have not disputed the contention that the Cruzans are a caring, loving family. The parents would not do anything that they felt in their hearts was not in their daughter's best interests. Who better than they know the mind and heart of their daughter?

Option 4 **Uphold the Missouri court's decision to deny the Cruzans' request and forbid the withholding of life-preserving medical treatment in all cases.**

The government has a strong interest in upholding the sanctity of life. Once you start backing away from this principle, you erode society's respect for life. The result will lead to all kinds of legal and moral problems.

For example, society does not consider suicide an acceptable course of action. Where do you draw the line between refusing life-sustaining treatment and committing suicide? How close do you want to get to a situation in which medical professionals, who are sworn to protect life, begin helping people to commit suicide? The possible abuses of such a situation foreshadow disastrous consequences, especially for the disabled elderly, whom society might consider as no longer useful.

The wishes of an individual who is incapacitated by an accident or disease can never really be known. People may *think* they know what course of action someone would prefer in a catastrophe, but no one knows for sure until an emergency happens. Circumstances may change. Medical advances may make possible recovery beyond what anyone ever expected; miraculous recoveries do occur. The fact that some individuals are incapacitated prevents them from reevaluating their situation. In view of that, the most humane and caring approach for the state would be to stand squarely on the side of life preservation.

THE DECISION IS YOURS.
WHICH OPTION DO YOU CHOOSE?

Option 1   **Reverse the Missouri court's decision. Grant the Cruzans' request to allow Nancy to die.**

Option 2   **Uphold the Missouri court's decision to deny the Cruzans' request due to lack of clear evidence as to Nancy's wishes.**

Option 3   **Uphold the Missouri court's principle of requiring clear and reliable evidence, but reverse its ruling in the *Cruzan* case.**

Option 4   **Uphold the Missouri court's decision to deny the Cruzans' request and forbid the withholding of life-preserving medical treatment in all cases.**

William Rehnquist, who became chief justice of the Supreme Court in 1986, considered whether Lester and Joyce Cruzan—and others in their situation— had the right to "pull the plug" on a terminally ill loved one.

The Supreme Court chose *Option 2*.

Chief Justice William Rehnquist announced the ruling of the Court on June 25, 1990. Only five of the nine justices backed the decision. Rehnquist took care to be diplomatic in what he acknowledged was a disturbing and delicate case.

Rehnquist and a majority of the Court agreed that, under the individual freedoms guaranteed by the by the Fourteenth Amendment to the Constitution, American citizens *do* have a right to refuse life-sustaining treatment. The state of Missouri could not interfere with this right. He went on to admit that the Missouri law "may have frustrated . . . the not-fully-expressed desires of Nancy Cruzan."

Yet Rehnquist argued that neither of these points was enough to support the Cruzan family's request. He argued that "the Constitution does not require general rules to work faultlessly." The general rule to which he referred was the Missouri law requiring clear and reliable evidence of a patient's wishes before removing life-support systems.

"The question," wrote Rehnquist, "is whether the United States Constitution forbids the establishment of this procedural requirement by the State. We hold that it does not." Rehnquist said that Missouri was within its rights to retain doubts as to whether the family members would make precisely the decision the patient would have wanted.

RESULT

The *Cruzan* decision originally sparked concern among groups advocating the right for individuals to control their lives and to die with dignity. By refusing to recognize requests from close family members regarding life support, the ruling seemed to deny that these rights existed.

But, in effect, the decision affirmed that the Fourteenth Amendment to the Constitution protected an individual's right to refuse treatment so long as clear and reliable evidence of the individual's wishes was available. This decision not only clarified a previously murky situation but also provided a specific way for people to avoid the type of agonizing situation in which the Cruzans were caught. The solution is a "living will." This document, signed and witnessed well in advance of the dying process, states the person's wishes regarding life support and right-to-die decisions. Most states have now authorized their courts and medical professionals to honor requests that are clearly spelled out in one of these wills.

Ironically, the Supreme Court ruling in *Cruzan* had little impact on the actual case. In the months following the decision, the Cruzan family was able to come up with new evidence regarding Nancy's wishes about life support in such a situation. On December 26, 1990, a Missouri county judge permitted medical authorities to remove the feeding tubes that sustained Nancy Cruzan's life. She died at age 33, two weeks after the tubes were removed.

AMENDMENTS TO THE U.S. CONSTITUTION

The Supreme Court cases discussed in this book center on the following amendments to the Constitution:

AMENDMENT I [1791]

Congress shall make no law respecting an establishment of religion, or prohibiting the free exercise thereof; or abridging the freedom of speech, or of the press; or the right of the people peaceably to assemble, and to petition the government for a redress of grievances.
(Schenck v. United States, and Board of Education v. Barnette)

AMENDMENT IV [1791]

The right of the people to be secure in their persons, houses, papers, and effects, against unreasonable searches and seizures, shall not be violated, and no warrants shall issue, but upon probable cause, supported by oath or affirmation, and particularly describing the place to be searched, and the persons or things to be seized.
(Roe v. Wade)

AMENDMENT V [1791]

No person shall be held to answer for a capital, or otherwise infamous crime, unless on a presentment or indictment of a grand jury, except in cases arising in the land or naval forces, or in the militia, when in actual service in

time of war or public danger; nor shall any person be subject for the same offense to be twice put in jeopardy of life or limb; nor shall be compelled in any criminal case to be a witness against himself, nor be deprived of life, liberty or property, without due process of law; nor shall private property be taken for public use without just compensation.
(Miranda v. Arizona)

AMENDMENT VI [1791]

In all criminal prosecutions, the accused shall enjoy the right to a speedy and public trial, by an impartial jury of the state and district wherein the crime shall have been committed, which district shall have been previously ascertained by law, and to be informed of the nature and cause of the accusation; to be confronted with the witnesses against him; to have compulsory process for obtaining witnesses in his favor, and to have the assistance of counsel for his defense.
(Gideon v. Wainwright, and Miranda v. Arizona)

AMENDMENT IX [1791]

The enumeration in the Constitution, of certain rights, shall not be construed to deny or disparage others retained by the people.
(Roe v. Wade)

AMENDMENT X [1791]

The powers not delegated to the United States by the Constitution, nor prohibited by it to the states, are reserved to the states respectively, or to the people.
(Roe v. Wade)

AMENDMENT XIII [1865]

SECTION 1

Neither slavery nor involuntary servitude, except as a punishment for crime whereof the party shall have been duly convicted, shall exist within the United States or any place subject to their jurisdiction.

SECTION 2

Congress shall have power to enforce this article by appropriate legislation.
(Schenck v. United States, and Brown v. Board of Education)

AMENDMENT XIV [1868]

SECTION 1

All persons born or naturalized in the United States, and subject to the jurisdiction thereof, are citizens of the United States and of the state wherein they reside. No state shall make or enforce any law which shall abridge the privileges or immunities of citizens of the United States; nor shall any state deprive any person of life, liberty or property, without due process of law; nor deny to any person within its jurisdiction the equal protection of laws.

SECTION 2

Representatives shall be apportioned among the several states according to their respective numbers, counting the whole number of persons in each state, excluding Indians not taxed. But when the right to vote at any election for the choice of electors for president and vice-president of the United States, representatives in Congress, the executive and judicial officers of a state, or the members of the legislature thereof, is denied to any of the male inhabitants of such state, being twenty-one years of age, and citizens of the United States, or in any way abridged except for participation in rebellion, or other crime, the basis of representation therein shall be reduced in the proportion which the number of such male citizens shall bear to the whole number of male citizens twenty-one years of age in such state.

SECTION 3

No person shall be a senator or representative in Congress, or elector of president and vice-president, or hold any office, civil or military, under the United States or under any state, who, having previously taken an oath, as a member of Congress, or as an officer of the United States, or as a member of any state legislature, or as an executive or judicial officer of any state, to support the Constitution of the United States, shall have engaged in insurrection or rebellion against the same, or given aid or comfort to the enemies thereof. But Congress may, by a vote of two-thirds of each House, remove such disability.

SECTION 4

The validity of the public debt of the United States, authorized by law, including debts incurred for payment of pensions and bounties for services in suppressing insurrection or rebellion, shall not be questioned. But neither the United States nor any state shall assume or pay any debt or obligation incurred in aid of insurrection or rebellion against the United States, or any claim for the loss or emancipation of any slave; but all such debts, obligations, and claims shall be held illegal and void.

SECTION 5

The Congress shall have power to enforce, by appropriate legislation, the provisions of this article. *(Brown v. Board of Education, Gideon v. Wainwright, Roe v. Wade, The University of California v. Bakke, and Cruzan v. Missouri)*

In 1990, more than 200 years after the signing of the U.S. Constitution, the Supreme Court justices based their life-or-death decision in the Cruzan *case on the Fourteenth Amendment. Pictured from left to right, Harry Blackmun, Anthony Kennedy, Byron White, Sandra Day O'Connor, William Rehnquist, Antonin Scalia, Thurgood Marshall, David Souter, and John Paul Stevens.*

SOURCE NOTES

Quoted passages are noted by page and order of citation:

p. 9: Laurence Baum, *The Supreme Court* (Washington, DC: Congressional Quarterly, 1985.)

pp. 12, 22: Harry Kalven, Jr., *A Worthy Tradition: Freedom of Speech in America* (New York: Harper & Row, 1988.)

pp. 13: J. Edward Evans, *Freedom of Religion* (Minneapolis: Lerner, 1990.)

pp. 20, 21, 30, 31, 32, 37 (1st, 2nd, 3rd), 82 (2nd), 88 (1st, 3rd), 136 (1st): Maureen Harrison and Steve Gilbert, eds., *Landmark Decisions of the United States Supreme Court* (Beverly Hills: Excellent Books, 1992.)

pp. 23, 33, 37 (4th), 47, 50 (2nd), 62, 69 (2nd), 73 (3rd), 107, 118 (2nd), 129 (1st): John Garraty, ed., *Quarrels that Have Shaped the Constitution* (New York: Harper & Row, 1987.)

pp. 49, 69 (1st), 119, 121: Don Lawson, *Landmark Supreme Court Cases* (Hillside, NJ: Enslow, 1987.)

pp. 50 (1st), 55 (2nd), 56 (2nd), 82 (1st), 88 (2nd), 89, 108, 114, 126 (1st, 2nd), 129 (2nd): Stephen Goode, *The Controversial Court: Supreme Court Influences on American Life* (New York: Julian Messner, 1982.)

pp. 55 (1st), 56 (1st), 73 (1st, 2nd), 75, 126 (3rd): Lee Arbetman and Richard L. Roe, *Great Trials in American History: Civil War to Present* (St. Paul: West, 1983.)

pp. 58, 94, 106 (1st): David O'Brien, *Storm Center: The Supreme Court in American Politics* (New York: W. W. Norton, 1986.)

pp. 63, 78 (1st), 96, 97: Ralph Mitchell, *Congressional Quarterly's Guide to the U.S. Constitution* (Washington, DC: Congressional Quarterly, 1986.)

pp. 78 (2nd), 80, 84, 85: Liva Baker, *Miranda: Crime, Law, and Politics* (New York: Atheneum, 1983.)

p. 106 (2nd): Marian Faux, *Roe versus Wade: The Untold Story of the Landmark Supreme Court Decision That Made Abortion Legal* (New York: Macmillan, 1988.)

pp. 134, 136 (2nd): Robert L. Risley, *Death With Dignity: A New Law Permitting Physician Aid-in-Dying* (Eugene, OR: The Hemlock Society, 1989.)

pp. 137, 143: Joan Biskupic, *The Supreme Court Yearbook* (Washington, DC: Congressional Quarterly, 1991.)

BIBLIOGRAPHY

Arbetman, Lee, and Richard L. Roe. *Great Trials in American History: Civil War to Present.* St. Paul: West, 1983.

Asch, Sidney. *The Supreme Court and Its Great Justices.* New York: Arco, 1971.

Baker, Liva. *Miranda: Crime, Law, and Politics.* New York: Atheneum, 1983.

Baum, Laurence. *The Supreme Court.* Washington, DC: Congressional Quarterly, 1985.

Bernstein, Richard B., and Jerome Agel. *Into the Third Century: The Supreme Court.* New York: Walker, 1989.

Biskupic, Joan. *The Supreme Court Yearbook.* Washington, DC: Congressional Quarterly, 1991.

Evans, J. Edward. *Freedom of Religion.* Minneapolis: Lerner, 1990.

Faux, Marian. *Roe versus Wade: The Untold Story of the Landmark Supreme Court Decision That Made Abortion Legal.* New York: Macmillan, 1988.

Garraty, John, ed., *Quarrels That Have Shaped the Constitution.* New York: Harper & Row, 1987.

Goode, Stephen. *The Controversial Court: Supreme Court Influences on American Life.* New York: Julian Messner, 1982.

Harrison, Maureen and Steve Gilbert, eds. *Landmark Decisions of the United States Supreme Court.* Beverly Hills: Excellent Books, 1992.

Lawson, Don. *Landmark Supreme Court Cases.* Hillside, NJ: Enslow, 1987.

Kalven, Harry, Jr. *A Worthy Tradition: Freedom of Speech in America.* New York: Harper & Row, 1988.

Mitchell, Ralph. *Congressional Quarterly's Guide to the U.S. Constitution.* Washington, DC: Congressional Quarterly, 1986.

O'Brien, David. *Storm Center: The Supreme Court in American Politics.* New York: W.W. Norton, 1986.

Peluso, Samuel. *To Live and Die With Dignity.* Long Branch, NJ: Vista, 1991.

Risley, Robert L. *Death With Dignity: A New Law Permitting Physician Aid-in-Dying.* Eugene, OR: The Hemlock Society, 1989.

Rubin, Eva R. *Abortion, Politics, and the Courts: Roe versus Wade and Its Aftermath.* Westport, CT: Greenwood, 1982.

Wilkinson, J. Harvie. *From Brown to Bakke: The Supreme Court and School Integration: 1954-1978.* New York: Oxford University Press, 1979.

INDEX

justices in, 86
Miranda warning, 90
Missouri State Supreme Court, 133, 137-138, 139, 140
Murphy, Frank, 36

National Association for the Advancement of Colored People (NAACP), 39-40, 49
National Council of Churches, 122
Nazis, 31, 51
New Jersey Supreme Court, 135-136
Ninth Amendment, 94, 96, 97, 98, 106
Nixon, Richard, 90, 91, 111

O'Connor, Sandra Day, 149
Oswald, Lee Harvey, 95

Planned Parenthood, 96-97
Plessy, Homer, 42-43
Plessy v. Ferguson, 40, 42-44, 47, 48, 49-50, 51, 52, 53, 115; overturning of, 54
police, job of, 82, 83-84, 88, 90, 92; and rights of accused, 78-80, 81-82, 85, 88-89
Powell, Lewis, 126-127, 129, 130
Powell v. Alabama, 64-65, 68, 73
precedents, legal, 8, 9, 30, 32, 40, 48, 65-66, 67-68, 78, 79-80, 88, 106; reversal of, in *Barnette* case, 36, 38; reversal of, in *Brown* case, 49, 51, 52, 54; reversal of, in *Gideon* case, 73

pregnancy, 96, 100, 101, 102, 106, 107
privacy, right of: and abortion, 100, 101, 102, 106, 107, 108, 110; guaranteed by the Ninth Amendment, 97, 98; and right to die, 135, 136

Quakers, 25
Quinlan, Joseph, 134-136
Quinlan, Karen, 134-136, 138
quotas, 118, 121, 122, 123-124, 127, 129, 130

rape, 65, 94, 96, 103
Reagan, Ronald, 111
Regents of the University of California v. Bakke, 115, 118, 125, 130; decision in, 126, 130; options of justices in, 125
Rehnquist, William, 108, 142, 143, 144, 149
religion, freedom of, 25, 27, 28, 29-30, 31, 38
reverse discrimination, 117, 118
"right to die," 134, 136, 138, 144
Roberts, Owen, 69
"Roe, Jane," 94, 96, 103, 112, *See also* McCorvey, Norma
Roe v. Wade, 94-95, 98, 105, 110, 111; decision in, 106-108, 109; options of justices in, 104
Roman Catholics, 25
Ruby, Jack, 95
Rutledge, Wiley, 36

Photo Credits

ABOUT THE AUTHOR

NATHAN AASENG is a widely published author of books for young readers. He has covered a diverse range of subjects, including history, biography, social issues, sports, health, business, science, and fiction. Twenty of his books have won awards from organizations such as the national Council for Social Studies, National Science Teachers Association, International Reading Association, Junior Library Guild, and the Child Study Association of America. Aaseng is the author of *Great Justices of the Supreme Court*, which was selected for the New York Public Library's prestigious 1994 Books for the Teen Age list, as well as *You Are the General, You Are the President, You Are the President II: 1800-1899*, and the forthcoming book, *America's Third-Party Presidential Candidates*. He lives in Eau Claire, Wisconsin, with his wife and children.